Letts

CAMBRIDGE
IGCSE® ENGLISH
as a Second Language

D1581801

Els
Van Geyte

527 565 04 7

Published by Letts Educational
An imprint of HarperCollins*Publishers*
The News Building
1 London Bridge Street
London
SE1 9GF

ISBN 978-0-00-821038-0

First published 2017

10 9 8 7 6 5 4 3 2 1

® IGCSE is the registered trademark of Cambridge International Examinations.
All exam-style questions, related example answers given on the website, marks awarded and
comments that appear in this book were written by the author. In examinations, the way marks
are awarded to questions and answers like these may be different.

Els Van Geyte asserts her moral right to be identified as the author of this work.

British Library Cataloguing in Publication Data
A CIP record for this book is available from the British Library.

Commissioned by Katherine Wilkinson
Project managed by Kate Ellis, Sheena Shanks
Edited by Anastasia Vassilatou
Proofread by Samantha Lacey
Cover design by Paul Oates
Cover photo © Andrii Muzyka / Shutterstock
Typesetting by QBS
Production by Natalia Rebow, Lyndsey Rogers and Paul Harding
Printed and bound in Great Britain by Martins the Printers

MIX
Paper from
responsible sources
FSC™ C007454

FSC™ is a non-profit international organisation established to promote the
responsible management of the world's forests. Products carrying the FSC
label are independently certified to assure consumers that they come from
forests that are managed to meet the social, economic and ecological needs
of present and future generations, and other controlled sources.

Find out more about HarperCollins and the environment at
www.harpercollins.co.uk/green

Contents

Contents

Introduction

Guidance for examination

Question types	What you have to do	Texts	Exam techniques
Reading questions a) Short text reading questions	Select details from a short text to answer questions.	Articles, blogs, webpages.	• Skim read the text and read the questions before you start writing. • Underline key words in the questions to help you focus on the information you are looking for. • Scan the text to find the details you need. • Keep your answers brief.
b) Longer multiple matching reading questions	Select details from a slightly longer, more demanding text. Match each question to one of the sections.	One continuous text divided into sections, or a number of shorter, related texts.	• Skim read the text and read the questions. • Underline key words in the questions to help you focus on the information you are looking for. • Read for detail and underline the information you need for your answer. • Avoid distractors: there may be something in one section or paragraph that seems to relate to a question, whereas the answer is in another section or paragraph. • Check that you have understood what is implied in the text, and that the information you have found is exactly what is asked for. Remember, you can use the letters A, B, C (and D) more than once.
Note-making questions	Select details from a short text to make notes and organise them under given headings.	An article, for example from a newspaper or magazine.	• Skim read the text, then read the headings before you select the details you need. • Read the headings carefully again as you make your notes. Double-check that each detail is one you really need. • Do not include examples, details or comments unless you are asked for them. • Remember: notes do not need to be in sentences – save time and keep them brief. • The bullet points show how many points you need to make; the length of the lines tell you how long each point should be. • Check that you have not included the same detail twice. • You do not need to use your own words for these notes.

Question types	What you have to do	Texts	Exam techniques
Summary-writing questions	Select details and organise them, in order to produce a summary of 80 words (Core) or 100 words (Extended) about one, two or three aspects of the text.	An article, for example from a newspaper or magazine; the article will be different from the one used for the note-making question.	• Skim read the text to get a general idea of how the information is organised. • Use skimming and scanning skills to find the details you need. • Use different colours to underline the different kinds of information you need. • Check that you have found exactly the right information; read the instructions at least twice, carefully. • If you have time, write brief notes under headings. • Check for repetition in your underlining or notes. • Check that you have not used any unnecessary words. If possible, reduce a phrase to one word. • Do not be tempted to add any ideas of your own when writing a summary. Use only details from the text in your own words as far as possible. • Stick to the word limit. • After you have made any changes to your summary, read through it again to check that it makes sense.

Question types	What you have to do	Exam techniques
Long writing questions	a) Produce a short composition to explain or describe, using pictures and/or prompts as a guide. The question includes information on purpose, format and audience. b) Produce a slightly longer composition in which you give an opinion about something, and argue for or against it. You need to develop your ideas further, adapt your style well to the reader and purpose, use more sophisticated vocabulary and structures, and use accurate grammar and punctuation. In this writing task you have to convince or persuade your reader.	• Read the question carefully. • Read it again and underline key words or phrases that tell you the form, reader and purpose so that you know the level of formality you need to use. • Look at any images or speech bubbles. Remember: these are just ideas you can use if you wish. If you can think of your own ideas, so much the better. Make sure they are relevant to the question. Using a concept map or outline plan before you start writing will help. • If you cannot think of your own ideas, it does not matter – you can still write a good text using one or more of the ideas you are given. • Make some very brief notes next to each prompt; perhaps use a concept map so that you have an idea of what to include. • You may be able to think of each prompt as one paragraph. • Underline key words in the bullet points that you have to use. • Start writing, and stick to the word limit. • Make sure you have a few minutes to check your work.

Question types	What you have to do	Texts	Exam techniques
Listening questions a) Shorter listening questions	Listen twice to a number of short extracts spoken by individuals, or brief conversations between two people, select details to answer two questions on each extract, and then write concise answers.	Recorded phone messages or brief dialogues.	• Remember to make good use of the pauses in the recordings. • Underline key words in the questions to help you focus on the information you need. • Try to work out where each conversation is taking place and what kind of language you will need to use. • Try to work out what kind of detail you should listen for, e.g. a weight or a time. • When you hear the recording again, take the opportunity to check that you have selected the right details. • Check that you have used a maximum of three words for each answer, not more. • Check that your spelling is accurate. If you do not know how to spell a word, guess by writing the sounds you hear.
b) Gap-filling questions	Listen twice to a longer text, spoken by a single person, and select details to complete gaps in a form or chart.	Speeches, radio talks, lectures.	• Remember to make good use of the pauses in the recordings. • Underline key words in the questions to help you focus on the information you need. • When the recording is being played for the first time, write as many of the answers as you can. • When you hear the recording again, take the opportunity to check that you have selected the right details. • Check that you have used only one or two words to complete the gaps, and that what you have written makes sense. • Check that your spelling is accurate. If you do not know how to spell a word, guess by writing the sounds you hear.

Question types	What you have to do	Texts	Exam techniques
c) Matching speaker to statement	Listen twice to six short extracts, spoken by six different speakers about the same topic, and match a list of speakers to a list of statements that they could have said.	Short monologues spoken by a variety of people of different ages.	• Use the pauses between the speakers to prepare yourself, in the same way as you did for the earlier listening questions. • Read the statements carefully. Make sure you understand them so that you can listen for the information or clues you need. • Underline key words in the statements that might help you focus on and identify the clues you need to answer the questions. • After you have heard the six speakers for the first time, there is a short pause. Use this time to decide which speakers you want to check or consider again. • After you have heard the recording again, there is a pause. During this time, check that you have not used the same letter twice. • Remember: one of the letters will not be used; there is an extra one to make you think hard.
d) Multiple-choice questions	Listen to a discussion or conversation between two speakers and then choose one correct answer out of three possible answers.	Semi-formal discussions and conversations between two speakers, sometimes with a host to introduce them.	• Use the pauses to prepare yourself, in the same way as you did for the earlier listening questions. • Read the questions and their three possible answers carefully. Make sure you understand them so that you can listen for the information or clues you need.
e) Note-completion questions (Extended)	Two parts: i) Listen to a talk and complete short notes. ii) Listen to a short conversation about the talk and complete short sentences.	i) A formal talk, lecture or presentation. ii) An informal discussion based on the same topic as i).	• Use the pauses to prepare yourself, in the same way as you did for the earlier listening questions. • Read the notes and the sentences carefully. Make sure you understand them so that you can listen for the details or clues you need. • Underline any key words in the questions that might help you focus on and identify the clues you need to answer the question.

Question types	What you have to do	Texts	Exam techniques
Oral assessment test	Have a 15-minute recorded conversation on a particular topic with an examiner, who may or may not be your teacher.	A wide variety of topics considered to be of interest to a broad range of people.	• After the warm-up, and during the preparation time, read the topic card carefully. • If there is anything on the card that you do not understand, ask. • Use your time effectively and think of some of the things you are going to say. • During the conversation, respond to the examiner's questions/ prompts with several ideas and sentences, not just single words or phrases. • During the conversation, use details and examples to develop your accounts and descriptions. • Use reasons and details to support your opinions. • Respond quickly to any change in the direction of the conversation.

Preparing effectively

1 Look after yourself

There are many simple ways to look after your brain and body so that you can perform at your best in exams. Exercise is vital if you want to have a healthy brain and a healthy body. Exercise is also known to be good for stress, mood and self-esteem and it aids learning. Sleep is also vital for both health and learning. Your sleeping brain is doing a lot of work for you!

Your brain needs the right choice of foods and plenty of liquid, ideally in the form of water. Brains don't work well when they lack fuel. However, when you are nervous, you may not feel like eating, so it is important to think about the kind of food that is both good for you, and that you will be happy to snack on in exam time.

2 Tackle pressure head on

Many factors affect how well your brain works on any particular day, and one of these is stress. In fact, stress can actually help you perform at your best, but if it builds up and you do not manage it properly, you can suffer from a number of negative side-effects: you may feel ill, perform less well, have mood swings and find it difficult to concentrate. Your brain will work better – and you will be healthier and happier – if you make it a habit to do de-stressing activities every day. Short-term strategies like listening to music and doing breathing exercises will help reduce the effects of stress.

Confidence is one of the biggest contributors to success. If you become more confident about your ability, it will be easier to deal with your nerves. The right mindset will help a lot; adopt an attitude that says: 'I'm up for this challenge. I will learn from failures. I will always bounce back. I will do better next time.'

3 Practise, practise, practise

Effective studying demands concentration. If you are serious about studying, switch off the phone, the TV, the radio and the email before you start your study session. It is better to study in short bursts, say for half an hour, and certainly for no more than an hour, and then to take a 'breather'. Get up from the desk, drink some water and walk about for a few minutes before getting back to your work.

There is a three-stage rule about learning: you need to go over topics three times, preferably in different ways, in order to fix the knowledge and understanding into your long-term memory. It is also important to space out your revision and to keep testing yourself. Testing is far better for you than just reading notes over and over again.

Finally, be confident and do your best. If you have studied hard, no one can ask for more!

This revision guide includes audio materials for you to listen to when you see the symbol

You will find the material online at: www.collins.co.uk/IGCSEESLrevision

Reading skills

You must be able to:

- skim and scan for facts and details
- understand what is implied but not directly stated.

Skimming and scanning

When there is a lot to read in very little time, you need strategies. Also skim and scan visuals and read any captions and labels.

Real life tip

People often neglect to read titles and subheadings. Make sure you always read them when you are skimming. They are extremely useful!

	What?	Why?	How?
Skimming	moving your eyes quickly over a text	• to get the overall meaning (the 'gist') • to decide what needs a closer reading	• read the title and subheadings • look at any pictures • read the beginning and end of each paragraph
Scanning	looking quickly	• to find specific information	• skim the text and then go back to where you think the information is

Understanding what is implied

To understand what a statement really means, to understand what is expressed subtly, not directly, you need to be able to 'read between the lines'.

Revision check

Words that go together

1. Cover the second column of the table. Which words complete these phrases from Chapter 1?

evolution	of	technology
uses	of	mobile phones
methods	of	communication
attitude	to	internet use

Nouns

2. Complete these words from Chapter 1.

w_b br_ws_r
_ppl_c_t_ _n
_q_ _pm_nt
m_ch_n_

Writing skills

You must be able to:

- collect and organise ideas before writing to explain or inform
- communicate your ideas clearly and effectively through writing
- use exactly the right words to express your ideas precisely.

Collecting and organising ideas before writing

Collecting ideas before writing is called 'brainstorming'. To do this effectively, you must be clear about the purpose of your writing. After brainstorming, you can organise your ideas using a concept map – a diagram in which you group your ideas into categories. The diagram shows your topic, the main ideas linked to it, and where the individual points from your brainstormed list belong.

Communicating your ideas clearly and effectively

Concept maps help you avoid writing irrelevant information and help you structure your text so that you can communicate your ideas effectively.

Using exactly the right words to express your ideas precisely

Having a large vocabulary will enable you to choose the exact word you need, e.g. appropriate technical language. To expand your vocabulary, work out the meaning of new words by looking for clues about them in the context. Then learn them!

> **Real life tip**
>
> To prepare for writing about a particular topic, read up on the topic first. This will help you become aware of the vocabulary you need. The most useful words are normally the ones used frequently.

Revision check

Words that go together

1. Cover the first column of the table. Which words from Chapter 1 go with the words in the second column?

word	processing
web	surfing
mobile	banking
social	networking

Words connected with smartphones

2. Complete these words from Chapter 1.

t_ _t m_ _ _ _ge
em_ _ _
v_ _eo
cal_ _ _ _r
_em_ _der

Speaking skills

You must be able to:

- communicate your ideas clearly, accurately and effectively
- keep a conversation going by developing ideas with details and examples.

Communicating your ideas clearly, accurately and effectively

Good communication happens when all the people in a conversation show an interest in it, take responsibility for it and help it go smoothly. This can be done in the following ways:

open body language	• leaning forward • nodding • smiling • not crossing your arms
good eye contact	• maintaining natural eye contact • not looking away
asking questions	• asking a question at the right moment • asking for clarification • asking for an opinion • encouraging your conversation partner(s)
listening carefully	• responding to what has been said, before adding your own ideas or questions • sympathising with what has been said
taking turns	• offering ideas • giving personal examples • not dominating the conversation

Keeping a conversation going

A conversation can be further developed by:

- giving examples for your own ideas
- explaining the examples a little.

Revision check

Words connected with computer data

1. Complete these words from Chapter 1.

> stor_ _ _
> b_ _ _up
> file tr_ _ _ _ _r
> syn_ f_ _ _s
> a_ _ _ss d_t_

Real life tip

When you watch a TV drama in English, pay attention to the conversations. The actors use appropriate body language, and the scriptwriters have written the dialogues so that people take turns to talk. Pay attention to the language. What types of questions do people ask? How do they show they are listening? How do they react to information' they hear? How do they give their opinions? How do they develop what they say? Make a note of useful phrases.

Listening skills

You must be able to:

- identify relevant information
- understand and select correct details and key question words
- understand what is implied but not directly stated in a more formal conversation.

Identifying relevant information, correct details and key words

In order to answer specific questions, you need to make sense of what you hear, and identify relevant information.

Before listening, skim read the questions so that you know what to listen out for. Underline any question words that show you need to listen out for a place name, a time, etc. Also underline any other key words that will help you focus on the answers that you have to listen out for. You may need to identify factual information, e.g. names of people or places, and numbers related to times, prices or dates.

Understanding what is implied but not directly stated

Information can be implied, especially in formal situations. This is because the situation may be sensitive and a speaker may be afraid of upsetting the listener if they say exactly what they think or feel.

Revision check

Definitions

1. Cover the second column of the table. Say each word in the first column aloud and then try to give a clear definition for it.

convenient	easy, or very useful or suitable for a particular purpose
confidential	meant to be kept secret or private
remarkable	striking or unusual
unwieldy	too heavy, large or awkward to be easily handled

Verbs

2. Complete these words from Chapter 1.

upl_ _ _
_bs_rb
e_it
d_mo_str_ _ _
c_ _sh

Chapter Test: Technology

1   **a)** Skim read the text below using the strategies you learned in this chapter.

b) Underline the key words in the following questions:

1 What is a self-driving car?

[1

2 Find three synonyms for 'self-driving' in the text.

[1

3 What are the advantages and disadvantages of self-driving cars?

[1

4 Why might we need more time to prepare before we use self-driving cars on the roads?

[1

c) Scan the text to find the answers to the questions in b).

1 ....

[1]

2 ....

[3]

3 ....

....

....

....

....

[11]

4 ....

[1]

Self-driving cars are robotic cars that do not need a driver. These driverless vehicles use technology such as radar and GPS to design a route and to ensure that people and objects are avoided. Self-driving cars already exist but are not used on public roads yet.

They are cheaper to make and use than our current cars, and they allow more people to 'drive', for example young people and disabled people. They could also help to reduce accidents, find parking solutions and give people more time to work or relax.

However, these automatic cars would require changes in the law. There would also be many social changes. People would need to be prepared to lose the fun aspect of driving, and people whose careers involve driving would most likely lose their jobs. Other worries are of a technical nature: people would need to be sure that they could trust a computer, and there are fears that criminals could exploit the technology so that it could be used for terrorism.

Perhaps we need more time to prepare for such a major technological change.

a) 🎧 **1** This task can be done by listening to the extract from a radio programme online, or reading the transcript of the audio below. If you listen to the audio, cover the transcript and then answer the questions.

Before listening or reading, consider the topic: 'Investing in technology in Africa'. What names do you think you will hear? Now listen and write:

1 the names of the places, people and companies you hear.

....

.... [6]

2 words and phrases related to technology.

....

.... [7]

b) Summarise the extract using some of your answers from 2a) to help you.
Write no more than 70 words. [3]

Transcript: Extract from a radio programme

While Africa is not typically thought of as a technology-focused continent, access to mobile phones and to the internet has increased rapidly there. This fact, along with economic growth and the expansion of educational opportunities, has led to investment opportunities for international companies – a development that President Kenyatta of Kenya has welcomed.

Large tech companies such as IBM and Microsoft have offices in Africa. IBM has a research facility in Nairobi, the capital of Kenya. This makes it possible to find solutions locally for some of the major problems still facing the African continent, such as lack of access to water, sanitation and energy. Microsoft also have offices in Kenya. Their focus is on developing the skills of young Africans – training them to create apps, for example – and on improving access to technology. They also encourage projects across Africa that improve access to technology and healthcare.

These companies clearly bring many benefits to Africa, and by encouraging economic development and providing technological solutions to do so, they also create more buyers for their own products. It is a win-win situation.

Total marks   /36

Reading skills

You must be able to:

- understand and pick out details from what you read in order to make notes.

Understanding and picking out details

When you need to pick out information from a text to make notes, read the text first so that you understand what is needed. If the text has subheadings, they may tell you where the information can be found.

Making notes

Keep notes short. Write words and phrases, not full sentences. Only include descriptions, opinions, or personal or emotional comments if you are specifically asked to do so.

	Do's	Don'ts
language	✓ words and phrases	✗ full sentences
content	✓ key points	✗ descriptions ✗ opinions ✗ emotional comments

Real life tip

Read a variety of texts in your own language. Notice that all texts have certain features in common: they have introductions and conclusions, and most texts give general information at the beginning and then become more specific. Being aware of how texts are structured will help you when you are looking for certain types of information.

Revision check

Definitions

1. Cover the first column of the table. What words from Chapter 2 do the definitions refer to? Check your answers in the first column. Then cover the second column and give the definitions for the words.

expedition	an organised journey that is made for a particular purpose
quest	a long and difficult search
travels	the journeys someone makes to places a long way from their home
voyage	a long journey on a ship or in a spacecraft
exploration	the study and testing of an area of land to try and find something

Nouns and adjectives

2. Complete these words from Chapter 2.

Nouns	Adjectives
disc_ _ _ _y	haz_ _ _ous
ex_ _ _ _ _er	r_mo_e
jo _ r _ _ y	mes_er_ _ing
te_ _ _tory	a_ _ess_bl_

Writing skills

You must be able to:

- collect and organise ideas and be ready to write for or against a point of view
- include your own ideas when writing to argue a point.

Collecting and organising ideas

Before you write, you need to think about your topic, make notes and organise them. If you then realise there are gaps in your knowledge, read more. You can use mind maps, webs or tables such as a KWL (**K**now/**W**ant/**L**earned) table:

K	W	L
What do I KNOW about the topic?	What do I WANT to know about the topic?	What have I LEARNED about the topic?
fill this in before reading	*fill this in before reading*	*fill this in after reading*

Real life tip

Become more informed about the world. Listen to the radio and watch TV about the issues that affect your country and the world. What are the topics that people disagree about? Can you develop your own point of view? The next step is to try and argue your point in English.

Including your own ideas when writing to argue a point

You need to show that you have considered different opinions before you give your own. Take a position and make it clear that you agree or disagree with something. Here is some useful language:

- I would like to suggest that ...
- I don't think we need to ...
- It is possible that ...
- I would argue that ...
- I am certain that ...
- I am convinced that ...
- It is undeniably true that ...

Revision check

Words that go together

1. Complete these phrases from Chapter 2. Use a preposition if necessary.

> set off .... an expedition
> be a benefit .... mankind
> research .... something
> acquire .... something
> prepare .... a journey
> spend money .... something
> be in awe .... somebody

Words that go together

2. Match the words in the first column with the words in the second column.

gaze	danger
face	something a success
generate	at the stars
declare	the paper
crease	electricity

Speaking skills

You must be able to:

- research and organise ideas for giving a talk or presentation
- plan an effective, individual opening for a talk or presentation.

Researching and organising ideas for a talk or presentation

When giving a talk or a presentation, your listeners need to understand the points you are making, so organise your ideas and express them clearly; don't jumble them together. Also, think about the expressions you are going to use.

To organise your ideas, you could colour code them and group them into themes to make them clear. Think about the most logical order in which to present your ideas.

Planning an effective, individual opening for a talk or presentation

The opening of a talk or presentation is very important as it needs to grab your listeners' attention. Here are some helpful ways to begin your talk:

Structure your talk	Connect with the audience	Make it interesting
• greet the audience • say what you are going to talk about	• use a rhetorical question • use the pronoun 'we'	• use facts and statistics • use an anecdote

Real life tip

Listen to a radio programme or podcast of a talk in English. Pay attention to the beginning. Which techniques does the presenter use at the start? Does he or she structure the talk, connect with the audience, or start with interesting facts or stories about the topic? Note down useful words or phrases that you could use yourself.

Revision check

Words that go together

1. Cover the second column of the table. Which words from Chapter 2 go with the words in the second column?

distant	land
medical	application
space	agency
unmanned	mission
oil	reserves
poisonous	fumes
imperial	court

Listening skills

You must be able to:

- understand and pick out facts when listening to short spoken texts
- understand and pick out facts when listening to a longer and more difficult text
- listen carefully and understand complicated instructions.

Understanding and picking out facts

You need to be able to identify facts when you listen to information. A fact can be proved to be true.

If you need to listen for specific words to fill in a form, remember to do the following:

- read the questions carefully to get an idea of the sort of information you should listen for
- fill in the gaps
- check that your answers make sense, especially grammatically.

Listening carefully and understanding complicated instructions

If you are being given instructions, listen carefully for facts and details. Listen also for instruction words. These are the imperative form of the verbs, the forms without 'to', e.g. 'leave', 'go'.

Real life tip

Practise your listening skills by using radio programmes or online sources. Choose programmes, videos or podcasts with factual content, e.g. current affairs or world issues, to practise listening for facts. First listen and make notes about all the facts you hear. These could be statistics, numbers, examples, etc. Then use your notes to make full sentences. Check these when you listen again.

Revision check

Nouns and adjectives

1. Complete these words from Chapter 2.

Nouns	Adjectives
l_ndsc_p_	_n_xpl_r_d
r_g_ _n	_mb_t_ _ _s
m_n_r_l d_p_s_ts	_ll_g_l
d_f_r_st_t_ _n	_rct_c

Chapter Test: Exploration

1 **List the following as fast as you can:**

a) five nouns or noun phrases related to space

.... [5]

b) six nouns or noun phrases related to the sea

.... [6]

2 This task can be done by listening to the extract from a presentation online, or reading the transcript of the audio below. If you listen to the audio, cover the transcript and then answer the questions.

Tick the strategies the speaker uses to make a good impression at the start of her presentation.

- She greets the audience. ☐
- She says what she is going to talk about. ☐
- She uses a rhetorical question. ☐
- She uses the pronoun 'we'. ☐
- She uses facts. ☐
- She uses statistics. ☐
- She uses an anecdote. ☐

[5]

> **Transcript: Extract from a presentation**
>
> Good morning, everybody. Today we are going to be looking at the life of the explorer Ferdinand Magellan. Many people know that his expedition was the first to sail around the world, but did you know that he did not actually complete the voyage himself? I would like to look at what happened during that famous voyage, but first we will learn a little about his early life.
> Magellan was born in Portugal in about 1480 but he was orphaned before he was ten …

3 **Read the statements below. Underline the facts and highlight the writer's personal opinions.**

a) Successful oil companies make money, but that does not mean that we need to worry about their activities.

b) Craters on the Moon and on Mars have been named after Magellan, which proves that he is the most important explorer in history.

c) I think we can say that Magellan was the first to go around the world, even though he was killed with a spear before his ship returned to Spain.

d) Sometimes people say Magellan was Spanish; but in fact, he was born in Portugal. [8]

4 Write these words in the correct column in the table.

| armada | cabin | crew | drill | flare | ivory | laquerware |
| leak | pearls | pirate | porcelain | well | | |

[12]

Oil exploration	The sea	Precious goods

5 Complete the two texts below, which are about reading and listening skills. Use one word in each gap.

[8]

Making notes when reading

When you make notes, keep them (a) .... Write words and phrases, not full (b) .... You will not normally be asked for details or (c) .... opinions, so don't include these in the notes. Include them only if you are specifically asked to do so.

Understanding and picking out facts when listening

You need to be able to select facts when you are (d) .... to information. A (e) .... is something that can be proved to be true. If you are listening for particular words to fill in gaps, do the following:

- read the questions carefully (f) .... you listen to the recording to give you an idea of the sort of information you should listen for.
- fill in the (g) .... and then check that the answers make sense, especially (h) ....

Total marks /44

Reading skills

You must be able to:

- select facts and details accurately from a written text
- understand the importance of units of measurement
- understand phrases about time
- use key question words to help find answers.

Selecting facts and details accurately

When you read a text, you often have to find the parts that contain the information you need, e.g. numbers and measurements in order to follow instructions.

Understanding the importance of units of measurement

Always include or check the units of measurement used in a text – they can make a big difference to the meaning.

Understanding phrases about time

Information about times and timings is important. You can easily pick out numbers in a factual text, but also look out for words used with them, e.g. 'about' or 'up to' – they show that the times are not exact.

Using key question words to help find answers

When you are asked questions about longer texts, find the key words in the questions. They tell you what to look for.

Question word	What you are looking for
When?	a time or date
Who?	a person or the name of a person
Where?	a place or the name of a place
Why?	a reason
What?	an object, event, idea or fact

Real life tip

If you go to a restaurant and the menu is in English, read the ingredients to learn more vocabulary related to food.

Revision check

Words that go together

1. Cover the first column of the table. Which words complete these phrases from Chapter 3?

a clove	of garlic
a serving	of rice and pasta
a chunk	of ginger
a tablespoon	of olive oil

2. Cover the first column of the table. Which words complete these phrases from Chapter 3?

stay	healthy
have	access to healthcare
be	a vegetarian
deprive	the brain of nutrients
use	salt sparingly

Writing skills

You must be able to:

- use a range of different kinds of sentences in your writing
- use simple, compound and complex sentences accurately
- include a range of appropriate linking devices and noun phrases to add detail and variety.

Using a range of different kinds of sentences

A sentence always starts with a capital letter and ends with a full stop (.), a question mark (?) or an exclamation mark (!). Sentences contain a subject and a verb.

Using simple, compound and complex sentences accurately; using a range of linking devices

To make your writing more fluent and interesting, use different types of sentences:

	Simple sentences	Compound sentences	Complex sentences
Ideas	one idea	two ideas, equally important	two ideas; one is more important than the other
Example	*You can record a personal best.*	*You may not break a world record **but** you can record a personal best.*	***When** you join our athletics club, we will work with you to improve your personal best.*

Including noun phrases to add detail and variety

You can make your writing more interesting or persuasive by using descriptive noun phrases. Compare how the longer noun phrase gives more detail and variety than the shorter one:

- *Many people get **skiing injuries**.*
- *Many people get **terrible skiing injuries**.*

Speaking skills

You must be able to:

- use a variety of structures when you are speaking
- link ideas using a range of connectives
- speak using abstract nouns and noun phrases to give variety to your sentences.

Using a variety of structures when you are speaking

Use a range of sentence structures to add interest to your spoken communication. Include simple, compound and complex sentences. For example, when presenting your point of view, use complex sentences to give your reasons and make a persuasive argument.

Linking ideas using a range of connectives

The connectives 'and', 'but', 'or' and 'so' can all be used to explain your ideas clearly. This is useful during discussions where you need to support your arguments.

Connectives	Relationship to the first idea
and	adds a similar idea
but	introduces a different idea
or	gives more possibilities
so	shows a result

Using abstract nouns and noun phrases for variety

Abstract nouns name things that cannot be touched. They can add interest to what you say. You can also use common noun phrases. Here are some examples:

Abstract nouns	Noun phrases
greed	a fizzy drink
fatigue	junk food
excitement	organic food
weakness	a positive state of mind

Revision check

Words that go together

1. Cover the second column of the table. Which words from Chapter 3 go with the words in the first column?

a balanced	diet
a vitamin	supplement
a food	group
an active	lifestyle
poor	health

Nutrients

2. Complete these words from Chapter 3.

prot_ _ns
ca_b_hy_ _at_s
_ _ls and f_ts
v_ta_ _ns
iner _s

Real life tip

To add variety to what you say, you need a wide vocabulary. Think about the last time you went to a doctor. What would you have said if the doctor only spoke English? What did the doctor tell you? Could you explain in English what you were told? If not, look up the phrases you need in a dictionary.

You must be able to:

- predict the kind of information you will hear, including units of measurement
- recognise high numbers when listening.

Predicting the kind of information you will hear

Before you listen to an audio recording, make notes about what you already know about the topic so that you can focus on the relevant information when listening. Also, think about what you might expect to hear. For example, you might expect units of measurement, e.g. for time, distances and weights.

Recognising high numbers when listening

You may have to distinguish and understand high numbers when listening. It is important to learn how high numbers are spoken and how they are written. Here are some examples:

Number in digits	Number in words
1 000	one thousand
10 000	ten thousand
100 000	one hundred thousand
1 000 000	one million
10 000 000	ten million
100 000 000	one hundred million
1 000 000 000	one billion (in the UK and US)

Number in digits	Number in words
12 400	twelve thousand four hundred
120 400	one hundred and twenty thousand four hundred
23 560 001	twenty three million five hundred and sixty thousand and one
2 356 000 001	two billion three hundred and fifty six million and one

Revision check

Words that go together

1. Cover the first column of the table. Which words complete these phrases from Chapter 3?

have	access to clean water
face	an uphill battle
save	lives
follow	a diet
bring	to the boil
cook	until tender

Words connected with cooking

2. Complete these words from Chapter 3.

br_wn
s_mm_r
s_ _s_n
s_rv_
fl_v_ _r

Chapter Test: Health

1 List the following as fast as you can:

a) four verbs that you might find in recipes

.... [4

b) four measurements that you might find in recipes

.... [4

c) four question words and the kinds of information they ask you to look for.

.... [4

2 Write these words in the correct column in the table.

| dairy   diabetes   fatigue   fortified cereal   junk food   nuts   obesity   poultry |
| vaccine   weakness |

Food	Health problems

[10]

3 Complete the phrases with 'do', 'go' or 'play'.

a) .... activities

b) .... Pilates

c) .... karate

d) .... basketball

e) .... ice hockey

f) .... running

g) .... exercise

h) .... rock climbing

i) .... skiing

[9]

4 Complete the text with suitable connectives. Do not use the same connective twice. [4]

I like outdoor activities, a) .... on rainy days I go to the gym
b) .... I dance in my living room. Nothing is better than a walk
in the woods, though, c) .... I try to do that at least once a
week d) .... most weeks I manage to do this.

5 **a)** 🎧 3 This task can be done by listening to the extract from a presentation online or reading the transcript of the audio below. If you listen to the audio, cover the transcript and then answer the questions.

Before listening or reading, consider the topic: 'World poverty'. What kinds of numbers do you think you will hear?

Now listen. Write down the numbers in words and as numerals. Include units of measurement where necessary.

.... [2]

.... [2]

.... [2]

.... [2]

b) 1 Listen or read again. Identify one simple, one compound, and one complex sentence.

....

.... [3]

2 What is the effect of each of these sentence types on the listener/reader?

....

.... [3]

3 What is the effect of using all three types of sentence structure in this short text?

....

.... [1]

c) Listen or read again.

1 Find the longest noun phrase. What is its effect on the listener/reader?

.... [2]

[1]

2 Find one abstract noun.

> **Transcript: Extract from a presentation**
> There are many issues facing the world today, but I can confidently say that there is one that is particularly relevant. The most important global issue is poverty. Have a look at the slides. The situation is worrying because 2.2 billion people live on less than the equivalent of $3.10 a day. Nearly 80 per cent of the extremely poor live in South Asia and Sub-Saharan Africa. That's 389 million people. This is a sad and worrying situation with severe consequences for the world as a whole.

Total marks /53

Reading skills

You must be able to:

- select relevant details to answer questions
- identify and select information/details from more difficult texts.

Selecting details to answer questions

When you read for detail, you need to know exactly what you are looking for. Break the text down into chunks. Then read each chunk, think about what it means and try to express the ideas in your own words.

Before you answer questions, check that you understand them. Then look for relevant words in the questions and scan for them in the text. Be careful: sometimes the word you are looking for is not in the text and you have to find another word or phrase with the same meaning.

Selecting details from more difficult texts

Approach these texts in the same way: try to answer the questions by finding relevant words or their synonyms in the text.

Do not worry about unfamiliar words. Keep reading – difficult words are often explained in the text or you may be able to work out their meaning from the context.

Revision check

Meaning

1. Cover the second column of the table. What is meaning of the underlined parts of the words in the first column?

neurobiologist	nerve
bilingual	two
monolingual	one
irrelevant	not

Words connected with education

2. Complete these words from Chapter 4.

| t_m_t_bl_ |
| _tt_nd_nc_ |
| c_ _rs_w_rk |
| d_sc_pl_n_ |
| q_ _l_f_c_t_ _n |
| c_rr_c_l_m |

Words with a similar meaning

3. Match the words in the first column with the words in the second column.

association	preoccupied
distracted	focus
concentrate	nerve ending
irrelevant	link
pain receptor	not connected

Writing skills

You must be able to:

- use appropriate vocabulary accurately and effectively when writing to inform or explain
- use a wide range of vocabulary for variety and clarity.

Using appropriate vocabulary effectively to inform or explain

Having a wide vocabulary that you really understand will help you write precisely to inform and explain, so build vocabulary banks associated with useful topics.

It takes time to learn words. When you first find a useful new word, this is called 'input'. When you know what the word means, you store it in your mind but this is usually only 'temporary storage'. When you come across the word again, you will try to 'retrieve' it – remember what it means. If you are successful, you have 'usage' of the word – you can use it appropriately in a sentence of your own. Finally, you achieve 'permanent storage'. This process takes time and you can get discouraged when you do not remember the meaning of a word, but try to see it as a game and do not give up.

Using a wide range of vocabulary for variety and clarity

It is important to keep your readers' interest, so avoid repeating the same words. Instead, make an effort to use a range of synonyms correctly.

> ### Real life tip
>
> Think about how your brain works and what types of intelligence you have. How can this help you learn vocabulary? For example, if you have musical intelligence, you could sing new words. Find what works for you, but you will still need to make an effort to achieve permanent storage.

> ### Revision check
>
> **Words that go together**
>
> 1. Cover the words in the second column of the table. Which words complete these phrases from Chapter 4?

focus	on	a task
pick	out	information
co-operate	with	your classmates
empathise	with	other people
be	in	search of answers
show concern	for	others

Speaking skills

You must be able to:

- speak clearly using the most effective words to explain and describe
- choose the correct vocabulary and level of formality for the listener.

Speaking clearly using the most effective words

In order to describe a person or a situation accurately and vividly, you need a large vocabulary. The most accurate choice of noun, verb, adjective and adverb will help you express yourself effectively, both when writing and when speaking.

Part of speech	Definition	Examples
noun	a word that refers to a person, thing or idea	*teacher, student*
verb	a word that expresses an action or a state	*study, be, look*
adjective	a word that describes a noun	*short, clever*
adverb	a word that adds information about an action	*study **hard**, walk **slowly***

Choosing the correct vocabulary and level of formality

When you speak about a topic, it is important to use vocabulary that is appropriate to the listener. Think about how formal you need to be in a certain situation and adapt your word choices. For example, you would use more informal words when you are speaking to younger people and more formal words when you are talking to teachers or talking about a technical topic.

Revision check

Formal and informal language

1. Cover the first column of the table. Find informal synonyms of the words in the second column. Then cover the second column and try to remember the formal words.

worry	anxiety
stop	inhibit
work together	co-operate
think about	ponder
not good enough	inadequate
out-of-date	obsolete

Listening skills

You must be able to:

- select details from different kinds of spoken texts
- use clues before you start listening, to help you understand a text
- understand what is implied but not directly stated in a formal talk.

Using clues to select details from different kinds of spoken texts

If you know the topic of a text, think about related vocabulary beforehand to help you understand it. Remember also to read the questions carefully and to underline key words that will help you find the answers. If you do not know any context beforehand, you will have to listen out for clues:

What can you find out about …	What can you focus on?	Possible clues
people?	Who is speaking? Are there several speakers?	different voices
roles?	What do the speakers do?	mention of jobs
a point of view or opinion?	What do the speakers feel or think about the issue?	language such as 'I think', 'I don't think that's true', 'actually', 'I agree with that, but …'
context?	Where or when is the conversation happening?	information about what has just happened, or is going to happen

Understanding what is implied but not directly stated

You sometimes have to listen 'between the lines' to understand what someone means but does not actually say. A simple comment or question may be a clue about something other than what is stated directly, e.g. how the speaker feels about something.

Revision check

Words connected with education

1. Cover the first column of the table. Which words from Chapter 4 go with the words in the second column?

school	curriculum
boarding	school
head	teacher
extracurricular	activity
corporal	punishment
private	tutor

Verbs

2. Complete these words from Chapter 4.

```
soc_ _lis_
_n_lys_
c_lc_l_t_
m_m_r_s_
r_c_gn_s_
p_n_sh
```

Chapter Test: Education

1   **Complete the text. Use one word in each gap.**

Ancient Egyptian Schools

In Ancient Egypt, wealthy families sent their sons to school by the age of four. Young girls, however, were not a) .... unless they were princesses or members of nobility, close to the Pharaoh, the highest power in Egypt. A young boy's b) .... was decided for him by his father before he started school and he was only educated in what would be useful to his future career. For example, if he was to become a potter, he would only c) .... how to make pots and pans. If he was to become a blacksmith, he would learn about metals and metal work. Being a scribe or a tax collector, which required reading and d) .... hieroglyphics, was highly valued. These professions paid well but the e) .... they required took several years to f) .... Young scribes had to spend long hours at their teacher's house copying out hieroglyphics on papyrus with a reed brush and ink. Mistakes on the papyrus, or even talking, could have meant the boys were g) .... by a rod on their backs.

[7

2   **Read the statements. Then write the same information in two different ways. The first one has been done for you.**

a) I think education is very important.

I value education highly.

In my opinion, very few things are more important than education.

b) Schools should prepare people for their careers.

....

....

c) Chemistry is not a subject that all pupils have to learn.

....

....

d) Education was very different in ancient times.

....

....

e) School is not just a place where students go to acquire knowledge.

....

....

[8]

3   **Read the statements. Then write the same information in a more informal way. The first one has been done for you.**

a) I value education highly.

I believe that education is very important.

b) She should have requested assistance from the teacher.

....

c) I regret that I cannot agree to that at this moment in time.

....

d) We would like to inform you that the show will commence shortly.

....

e) We were forced to reject the idea for numerous reasons.

....

f) Apologise to your grandmother without delay.

.... **[5]**

4 **a)** Write definitions for the following parts of speech.

    1 noun: ....

    2 verb: ....

    3 adjective: ....

    4 adverb: .... **[4]**

b) Find the following in the text below:

    1 four nouns .... **[2]**

    2 four verbs .... **[2]**

    3 two adjectives .... **[1]**

    4 four adverbs. .... **[2]**

Brain facts

Did you know that the brain is made up of about 75 per cent water and weighs around three pounds? Strangely, there are absolutely no pain receptors – nerve endings – in the brain. This means that although you may think you are experiencing pain in the brain, the brain itself can feel no pain.

Memory is formed by associations, so to promote memory when studying we should create associations – linking one idea with another. 'A for apple' is an example of an association that we learn early on in life when we begin to learn our ABC. We learn to link together the word 'apple' with the letter 'A' and probably a picture of an apple. This can be done in any language: children who learn letters, characters or symbols in their own language will make similar links and associations.

Remarkably, children who learn two languages before the age of five have a different brain structure from children who learn only one language.

Total marks /31

Reading skills

You must be able to:

- use text features to pick out key points, facts and details
- find related details in a text in preparation for summarising.

Using text features to pick out key points, facts and details

Texts often have features that help to organise the information, to make it easier to find, and to make the texts look more interesting. When you are reading any text, you should use all its features to help you understand it. They can help you find the information or detail you need quickly.

Real life tip

Challenge a friend to a game. You each need to choose a geography or science textbook that you own. Who can find an example of each of the following first: a photo, an illustration, a diagram, a caption, a bulleted list?

Text features typical of non-fiction texts:

- headings
- photos and illustrations
- tables and diagrams
- fact boxes
- captions

- bold/capital letters
- bulleted lists
- maps
- quotations
- navigation bars

Finding related details in preparation for summarising

When you want to write a summary of a text, it is useful to find and organise related details.

Revision check

Measurements

1. Cover the first column of the table. Which nouns from Chapter 5 do the descriptions in the second column refer to?

weight	the amount that tells you how much something weighs
length	the amount that tells you how long something is
speed	the amount that tells you how fast something goes

Words that go together

2. Cover the second column of the table. Which words from Chapter 5 go with the words in the first column?

protected	status
outdoor	pursuit
coastal	waters
predatory	fish
scientific	survey
apex	predator
migration	patterns

Writing skills

You must be able to:

- use paragraphs correctly
- link ideas to write a smooth-flowing paragraph
- use a variety of connectives to write a summary.

Using paragraphs correctly

A paragraph is a number of sentences that express one main idea.

What does it do?	Why do we use paragraphs?
A new paragraph usually introduces a new idea.	Paragraphs break up the text and make it easier to read.
Often there are one or two supporting details in a paragraph which give more information about the main idea.	They organise information into meaningful chunks.

A topic sentence often appears at the start of a paragraph. It captures the meaning of a paragraph or a group of paragraphs.

Linking ideas using a variety of connectives

To write well, you need to join different ideas together so that they read smoothly. You can do this by using a variety of connectives, which are words or phrases that join sentences together, e.g. 'and', 'but', 'so', 'although', 'because', 'in spite of' and 'in contrast'.

Connectives not only link ideas within a paragraph, they also link one paragraph to another.

Writing a summary

Summarising is a skill we all use every day. A good summary:

- includes the main points/ideas
- uses your own words
- is ordered logically.

It does not include your opinions.

Revision check

Words that go together

1. Cover the first column of the table. Which words complete these phrases from Chapter 5?

cross	the finishing line
score	a point
break	a world record
win	a medal
hold	a tournament

Nouns

2. Complete these words from Chapter 5.

_ _dience
a_ _ _ _vement
v_ _ _ory
media c _ _ _rage
ful_ _ _ment
s_ _olarshi_

Speaking skills

You must be able to:

- build a conversation by asking and answering questions
- be an active listener and add new ideas.

Building a conversation by asking and answering questions

Asking questions helps to build a conversation. Use them to:

- open a conversation
- ask a question back
- change the direction of a conversation
- request information or an opinion
- develop an idea
- ask someone to repeat something.

When replying, avoid short answers. Instead, give examples to illustrate your points. Useful phrases are: 'for example', 'for instance', 'to give you an example'.

When you are asked a 'closed' question, requiring a 'Yes' or 'No' answer, you can add extra information, e.g. about where, when or how something was done. It is also natural to ask a question back.

Question	What it asks for	Example
What ...?	information	*What did you see/hear?*
What/How ...?	an opinion or response	*What did you like most?* *How did it make you feel?*
Why ...?	reason for an opinion	*Why do you think this?*

Being an active listener and adding new ideas

Good conversations happen when people listen actively, take turns and develop the discussion. Do this as follows:

- listen carefully
- show that you have listened by rephrasing what your partner has said
- give your own opinion
- ask a question back.

Revision check

Words that go together

1. Cover the second column of the table. Which words complete these phrases from Chapter 5?

get knocked	out	of a competition
push yourself	to	the limit
be beaten	on	penalties
audition	for	a show
be reduced	to	tears
be intent	on	winning
be judged	on	your talent

Listening skills

You must be able to:

- understand and pick out facts in short informal dialogues
- recognise and understand opinions in short informal dialogues
- recognise and understand facts and opinions in longer, more formal dialogues.

Understanding and recognising facts and opinions

It is important to understand the difference between facts and opinions:

	Definition	Examples
fact	A fact is something that can be proved.	*This is a phone.*
opinion	An opinion is a belief or judgment that is not based on fact or knowledge and that cannot be proved.	*This is a **wonderful** phone.* *This is **the best** phone.*

You can often tell the difference between a fact and an opinion by looking out for adjectives, e.g. 'wonderful' and 'best', as these are often used to give an opinion about what something is like. Numbers and percentages, however, often indicate that something is a fact.

When speaking, people rarely introduce their opinions with 'I believe …' or 'I think …' but will often try to convince you of their opinions by mixing facts with opinions, or by telling you why they think something is useful, beautiful, good, etc.

Real life tip

Find a programme to watch that features a debate or a political speech. Notice how the speakers try to convince listeners of their point of view. Draw two columns: one for facts and one for opinions. Make notes in the columns. Did you hear more opinions than facts? Did that affect whether you were convinced about what the speakers were saying? If you become a critical thinker, you will be able to identify opinions and challenge these if you want to, e.g. by stating facts.

Revision check

Words connected with technology

1. Complete these words from Chapter 5.

    tou_ _sc _een
    an_ _ _ _a
    f_ _ture
    han_ _ _ _
    sub_ _ _iption
    pr_dict_ _ _ te_ _ing

1 **a)** 🎧 **5** This task can be done by listening online to the extract from a speech about dealing with pressure, or reading the transcript of the audio below. If you listen to the audio, cover the transcript and then answer the questions.

Listen to or read the extract. Underline five facts that are mentioned. Include at least one example of a truth that everyone accepts as well as facts that include numbers.

[5

b) Listen or read again. Highlight one opinion.

....

[1

c) Read the transcript (again). Which connectives are used?

....

[4

2 **a)** Divide the text below into four paragraphs. Indicate where each paragraph ends with two short lines (//).

[4

> **Transcript: Extract from a speech**
> Exams are seriously stressful! They're an important part of your education and help determine the direction your life will take. But what if you struggle to answer the questions, your mind goes blank, or you haven't revised a particular topic? Forget spiders, snakes and heights. One of our greatest fears is failure. If we dwell on the consequences of underachieving, the thought of failure becomes more and more terrifying. This can shake your confidence pretty badly, make you feel more nervous and make taking an exam a bit more difficult. The great news is that you can change the way you think. World-class athletes know this. Four whole years of training go into an Olympic performance. Can you imagine the pressure that athletes are under as they step out into the stadium and ready themselves for a performance of a lifetime? But world record breakers and gold medallists aren't constantly thinking 'What if?' and that terrifying fear of failure. These athletes are nervous when the buzzer or starting gun sounds, but confident that if they give it everything they have, then the gold medal is theirs. Elite performers expect to succeed; they don't try not to fail! They go out there ready to show the world what they can do. Sport psychology is used to help athletes cope with these enormous pressures, putting all their energy into a winning performance. A large proportion of an athlete's training is mental. Just like those world-class athletes, you can learn how to respond successfully to the stress of taking exams. So, to successfully control exam nerves, I'm going to discuss two things: firstly how and why we get nervous, and secondly, coping strategies to reduce anxiety levels and build your confidence.

b) Summarise the extract but do not include the information in the last sentence. Write 40–60 words. Include the main points and the speaker's opinion. Remember to use your own words and do not include details or your own opinion.

[4]

3 Choose the two best answer options to each of the questions below.

a) Do you play any sports?

1 No, I don't really.

2 No, I'm not allowed to. When I was little, I needed operations on my eye and I have to be careful not to hurt it. There aren't many sports where you can't be hit by a ball, another object or a player!

3 No, I'm not very sporty. I'm rather clumsy and not very strong, but I like watching sports. I'm into rugby and adventure sports and I admire the athletes who take part in them. Maybe I'm most interested in the sports that I know I really couldn't do myself!

4 No, I don't really. I have three brothers and we often visit Portugal because we have family there.

b) Do you like listening to music?

1 I love listening to music. I always have my headphones on when I go out. I get so into it that I have to make sure I don't forget where I'm going.

2 Yes. Music is nice.

3 No. I played sports when I was little but I didn't learn to play an instrument.

4 I like listening to music. People sometimes ask me what I like to listen to but I don't have any favourite styles. I just play music to match the mood I'm in that day, so it could be anything – classical, heavy metal or pop. So yes, anything really.

[4]

Total marks /22

Reading skills

You must be able to:

- select facts from a range of texts which also contain personal opinions
- recognise the language used to introduce facts and straightforward personal opinions.

Selecting facts from texts which contain personal opinions

It is important to be able to pick out descriptive information, opinions and facts when you are reading texts. Remember: you can prove that a fact is true; an opinion is a point of view, which people may agree or disagree with.

Recognising the language used to introduce facts and personal opinions

You have to study a text containing facts and opinions carefully to interpret the information in it. Look out for language clues and think about whether what the text says can be proved or whether it is the opinion of the writer.

Opinions are often given in personalised language with phrases such as 'for me' and 'I find'. Facts may express an exact amount of something that can be measured or counted, and so proved.

Revision check

Definitions

1. Cover the first column of the table. What words from Chapter 6 do the definitions refer to? Check your answers in the first column. Then cover the second column and give the definitions for the words.

Words connected with jobs

2. Complete these words from Chapter 6.

> m_ _ _ging dir_ _ _ _r
> we _ d_ _ _gner
> sup_ _vi_ _r
> se_ _-em_ _oy_ _
> _ _exib_ _ w_rk

independent	used to describe people who can see what needs to be done and will take risks to make it happen
technical	used to describe people who enjoy seeing how things work and being involved in the practical details
managerial	used to describe people who are good at organising people and processes
creative	used to describe people who have lots of ideas and who are always thinking of new products

Writing skills

You must be able to:

- use the appropriate tone and style when you are writing a letter or a magazine article.

Using the appropriate tone and style

Your writing style will depend on the situation and the people you are writing to or for, e.g. a letter to a friend will be different from one to a stranger in content, vocabulary, sentence structure and punctuation.

Formal and informal writing

	Formal writing	Informal writing
words	formal (e.g. *role, position*)	informal (e.g. *job*)
phrases	formal (e.g. *I hope you are well.*)	informal (e.g. *How's things?*)
word forms	full forms (e.g. *do not*)	contractions (e.g. *don't*)
sentences	full	informal punctuation (e.g. dashes, bullet points)
exclamation marks	none	for emphasis
idioms	not many	yes

Formal letters

	Start	End
If you know the name:	Dear + person's name	Yours sincerely
If you do not know the name:	Dear Sir/Madam	Yours faithfully

Job applications

- Start the letter correctly.
- Use the appropriate tone and vocabulary, e.g. formal words, full sentences and forms.
- Use a clear paragraph structure.
- Use a sophisticated tone.

Articles

- Think of your readers and use the right tone (formal or informal).
- Use appropriate structures, e.g. full forms for formal articles, contractions for informal ones.
- Use appropriate language, e.g. descriptive and informative phrases, sophisticated vocabulary.

Revision check

Formal and informal language

1. Cover one of the columns. Which formal/informal phrases mean the same?

Formal	Informal
I am keen on …	I love …
I would prefer …	I'd prefer …
How are you?	How's things?
I am looking forward to it.	Can't wait!
many/much	loads of

Words that go together

2. Cover the first column of the table. Which words complete these phrases from Chapter 6?

apply	for a job
get	a job
train	for a job
earn	money
make	a difference

Speaking skills

You must be able to:

- pronounce words and speak clearly to be understood in a conversation
- speak up confidently and clearly.

Pronouncing words clearly

Participants in a conversation need to speak and pronounce their words with clarity; otherwise, their message may be passed on incorrectly or not at all.

It can be difficult to pronounce words correctly in a formal situation such as a job interview or an exam. Try not to speak too fast when you are nervous and pronounce your words as clearly as possible.

Speaking up confidently and clearly

In confident speech, words become connected. It is not always possible to hear where one word ends and the other one begins: if one word ends in a consonant and the next begins with a vowel, they will sound like one word. This is normal, so do not try to speak word by word; just make sure you pronounce everything you say clearly.

Think about what you may be asked in a conversation ahead of time. This way, your answers will be more confident and clear. It is a good idea to practise and to record yourself speaking in English. This will help you improve your clarity.

Revision check

Definitions

1. Cover the first column of the table. What word do the definitions refer to? Check your answers in the first column. Then cover the first column and try to give the definitions for the words.

keen	wanting to do something very much
confident	being certain that things will happen in the way that you want them to; sure about your own abilities or ideas
embarrassed	feeling shy, ashamed or guilty about something
talented	having a natural ability to do something well

Listening skills

You must be able to:
- predict to help you understand and select details
- select details to make notes or fill in forms when listening to a range of texts.

Predicting to help you understand and select details

When you listen to longer texts, you may have to pick out specific details. It is very helpful to predict the kind of information you might hear. For example, if you are making notes, be clear about which headings you will use. This will help you listen out for the information you need.

Selecting details to make notes or fill in forms

If you are asked to fill in a form, read it through first and consider the types of information you will need to complete, e.g. names, ages and places. Make sure you listen carefully for these. The information you put in the form must make sense. Unless you are asked for full sentences, write a word or short phrase.

Real life tip

Become familiar with spoken texts. Choose a radio or TV programme or a podcast and try to predict what you will hear. For example, imagine you will be listening to a programme about working hours around the world. You could write down the following headings: places, times, numbers of hours, job titles. Then listen and write details under the headings. This will help you select details to make notes.

Revision check

Words that go together

1. Complete these phrases from Chapter 6.

> come .... with new ideas
> get on .... people
> .... risks
> set .... a business
> .... your own business
> be rushed .... your feet

Words connected with business

2. Complete these words from Chapter 6.

> inves_ _ _
> entrepre_ _ _ _
> indu_ _ _ _
> f_ _ding
> p_ _fit

1 **a)** You will hear a talk at a youth conference. First, read the extract from the introduction to the conference. Use the information in the extract to write some headings for the notes you will make during the talk.

> Welcome to our annual youth conference. In this first talk, you will hear about how people have different attitudes to studying, work and life in general. Two main ways of dealing with life will be discussed, and you will have the opportunity to learn how to approach your own life in order to be successful at school and in your future career.

b) 🎧 6 🎧 This task can be done by listening to the extract online, or reading the transcript of the audio below. If you listen to the audio, cover the transcript and then answer the questions. Listen to or read the talk. While you listen/When you read, make notes under your headings.

c) Check that your headings are correct and decide if you need any other headings or subheadings.

d) Listen or read again and write any missing details in note form.

e) Use your notes to answer the following questions:

1 What is a mindset?

.... **[1]**

2 What is the difference between a fixed mindset and a growth mindset?

....

.... **[2]**

3 Why do some people have a fixed mindset?

.... **[1]**

4 What mindset should you adopt? Why?

....

.... **[2]**

5 What mindset do you have? Will you make any changes? Would it be difficult to make changes?

....

.... **[1]**

f) Read the transcript of the talk to check your answers in 1e).

Transcript: Extract from a talk

Your attitude to studying, and to work and life generally, matters. If you approach a task reluctantly and feel negative about it, it is unlikely to go well. If you are positive and get on with it, it will be an altogether more satisfactory experience. Professor Carol Dweck of Stanford University has done a lot of work in this field, confirming what many have always known, but also exploring *why* people adopt a certain mindset and the *consequences* of their choice.

Many people have a *fixed* mindset. They fear failure and avoid challenges. If they do not pass a test, they find plenty of excuses but will be unwilling to confront head on the simple fact that they didn't work hard enough. They might well be scared of working hard, since they think this is something intelligent people shouldn't have to do. They don't want to appear hard-working because that would mean admitting they aren't intelligent.

Of course, this is nonsense, but people think this way because parents and teachers praised them too much when they were young, telling them so often that they were clever or good at something that they find it a shock when, as they get older, they realise some things are actually quite hard and an adult won't always be there to praise them or even to do it for them.

Whether it is at age 12 or 17 that you realise success doesn't always come easily, you'll find a fixed mindset crippling. It will tell you to sidestep the challenge, to settle for the easy life, perhaps even to give up altogether. And what a shame that would be!

The alternative is to cultivate a *growth* mindset. If you can build this sort of attitude, you will look positively on challenges. You won't fear failure but see it as an opportunity to discover what you have to work harder at.

You won't avoid people who seem to be better than you. You will observe what they do and practise so that you can perform skills as well as they do. You will understand that while there are undoubtedly very clever and gifted people in the world, they all work very hard at being good at what they do. This includes students who win prizes at school. They may not admit it, but as well as being clever, they almost certainly study as much as anyone.

If you have a growth mindset, you will get more satisfaction from success because, having worked hard, you will have earned it. From every failure you will emerge, not depressed, but pleased that you have learned something. You won't give up. You will get there. And what's more, you will be a happier person.

So, think about mindset. Discuss it with your teachers and parents or guardians. Even if it doesn't come naturally to you, you can work at it and move yourself from a fixed to a growth outlook on life. It's a no-brainer. Don't be fixed, go for growth. It might be the most important thing you do – ever!

Total marks   /7

Reading skills

You must be able to:

- understand texts containing pie charts and bar graphs
- understand what is implied but not directly stated in a piece of text.

Understanding texts containing pie charts and bar graphs

It is a useful skill to understand charts and graphs. They appear frequently in newspapers and magazines and are widely used in school subjects, such as Geography. In the world of work and further study, you may use charts and graphs when giving presentations or need to understand them in anything you read.

Pie charts:	Bar graphs:
• are circular, like a pizza, with wedges • represent percentages; the whole pie is 100 per cent and each wedge is a part of that • help us break down information into categories and see how each contributes to a bigger picture • may have a legend that explains what each wedge represents.	• have bars of equal width but different heights • are used to compare categories of data, summarise generalisations or illustrate a trend or pattern • have an x-axis (the line along the bottom) and y-axis (the line up the side) • may have a legend that explains what each bar represents.

Understanding what is implied but not directly stated

When writers do not state things directly, you have to work out their feelings or attitudes. To help you do this, think about the vocabulary choices the writer has made: do the words and phrases express positive or negative attitudes?

Real life tip

Find a pie chart or bar graph in a magazine or textbook. To understand better what it shows, ask yourself if the information it contains could also be shown in a different type of visual. Why (not)?

Revision check

Words connected with the environment

1. Complete these words from Chapter 7.

> c_rb_n f_ _tpr_nt
> r_c_cl_ng b_n
> gl_b_l w_rm_ng
> _m_ss_ _ns
> gr_ _nh_ _s_ g_s
> d_for_st_t_ _n
> m_th_n_

Writing skills

You must be able to:

- use details to develop ideas when writing descriptions
- make descriptive writing convincing using the five senses.

Using details to develop ideas when writing descriptions

To describe experiences or issues well, you need to use details. One useful technique is to start with general information and then give specific details. Examples, facts and images will help your writing come to life and engage your readers.

Examples	Type of detail
My family's life revolves around water: **finding or buying it, conserving it or storing it, dreaming and thinking about it.**	examples/detail
When he was a boy, **two million tons of** sewage were dumped into the water.	factual information

Making descriptive writing convincing using the five senses

When you describe an experience, use the senses of sight, sound, smell, and even touch and taste to help the reader enter your world. A great way to make your writing more convincing is to use vivid adjectives and well-chosen nouns.

Examples	Type of detail
He could enjoy **soothing, warm** baths or **cool, refreshing** showers.	vivid adjectives added to nouns
I can enjoy **the beauty of** the forests, the **winding** rivers and the **scent of evening rain on** blossom.	description of what can be seen and smelled

Revision check

Verbs of the senses

1. Cover the first column of the table. Which verb, *see*, *hear*, *taste*, *feel* or *smell*, completes these phrases?

see	a dazzling light
feel	a soothing touch
taste	flavoured water
hear	slapping water
smell	scented candle

Nouns and noun phrases

2. Complete these words from Chapter 7.

```
fr_shw_t_r s_ _rce
cont_m_n_t_ _n
_nd_str_ _l w_st_
pli_ht
d_s_l_n_t_ _n plant
```

Speaking skills

You must be able to:

- express your ideas clearly using the correct verb tenses
- respond clearly, accurately and effectively to others in a conversation
- communicate your ideas clearly and confidently in a more formal talk.

Expressing your ideas clearly using the correct verb tenses

The simple present tense and the present continuous tense refer to facts that are current or true over a long period of time. The first verb in every sentence *must* agree with the subject of the sentence.

	What does it describe?	How is it formed?	Example
Simple present	routines, facts, likes and dislikes or attitudes and opinions	infinitive without 'to', with an 's' ending for a verb after he/she/it	*The burning of fossil fuels **leads** to air pollution and **creates** greenhouse gases in our environment.*
Present continuous	events happening at the moment of speaking or at the present period of time	the present tense of 'to be' and the main verb with an 'ing' ending	*The water table **is shrinking** in many parts of the world.*

Responding clearly, accurately, effectively and confidently

In an informal conversation, you need to listen and then respond clearly, accurately and effectively.

In order to give a speech that flows well and naturally, you need to spend time planning it and making sure your sections link together. Also, be clear about your facts and key words and what they mean.

> **Revision check**

Words that go together

1. Cover the second column of the table. Which words from Chapter 7 go with the words in the first column?

outer	space
forest	fire
human	being
odourless	gas

endangered	species
factory	smoke
respiratory	disease
long-term	consequences
heart	disease
lung	cancer
acid	rain
air	pollution
carbon	dioxide

Listening skills

You must be able to:

- understand the connections between ideas, opinions and attitudes
- understand what is implied but not directly stated during an interview.

Using key words to answer multiple-choice questions

Always read the questions you have to answer before listening. Identify both the question words (e.g. 'Who', 'When'), and the key words. When you hear the key words, you will know that the answer is likely to be given soon.

Sometimes, you have to be especially alert and listen out for words and phrases whose meaning is the same as or similar to key words in the questions. To identify these words or phrases, you need to have a very good vocabulary.

Understanding what is implied but not directly stated

Sometimes you have to understand what people mean from what they imply. You have to pick up on clues, so listen out for these.

> **Real life tip**
>
> Remember that writers often explain an unusual or difficult word by using a synonym (i.e. a word or phrase that means the same) when referring to something again. Therefore, you should usually be able to find words or phrases in texts that explain difficult words. If you practise looking for synonyms, you will find it easier to hear them when you are listening to spoken texts.

> **Revision check**
>
> **Words that go together**
>
> 1. Cover the first column of the table. Which words complete these phrases from Chapter 7?
>
> | harbour | life |
> |---------|------|
> | pose | a danger |
> | burn | fossil fuels |
> | trample | crops |
> | tackle | an issue |
> | shrug | your shoulders |
>
> **Nouns**
>
> 2. Complete these words from Chapter 7.
>
> c_ns_rv_t_ _n_st
> _ct_v_st
> c_rn_v_r_
> pr_d_t_r
> p_ _ch_r

Chapter Test: Environment and wildlife

1 List the following as fast as you can:

a) two jobs that relate to the protection of the natural environment

.... [2]

b) four problems of the natural world caused by human beings.

.... [4]

2 Complete the interview on a radio programme with the correct simple present or present continuous form of the verbs in brackets.

Allison:	Good morning, listeners. You're listening to Radio Ramona. Welcome to today's programme: 'Our environment, our future', in which we'll be talking about recycling. Did you know that most Western nations (a) .... (recycle) between one- and two-thirds of their waste? This is mainly due to an increase in the number of recycling plants. These places (b) .... (collect) and (c) .... (treat) glass, aluminium and paper so that people can use them again. Today we've come to talk to Leon, who (d) .... (work) at Ramona's only recycling plant. Hi, Leon. What exactly (e) .... (you / do) here?
Leon:	Hello, Allison. Well, what I do is, um, every day we (f) .... (get) deliveries of recyclable materials. Every household (g) .... (have) a special bin for recyclable household waste, and we (h) .... (collect) these bins and (i) .... (bring) them here. Unfortunately, some of the rubbish (j) .... (not be) recyclable, so we have to sort it when it gets here. As you can see, that's what I (k) .... (do) at the moment. I (l) .... (sort) through these items and I (m) .... (put) them in this container. This kind of plastic and those boxes over there can't be recycled. And I (n) .... (do) this every day.

[14]

3 **a)** 🎧 7 This task can be done by listening to the extract from an interview online, or reading the transcript of the audio below. If you listen to the audio, cover the transcript and then answer the questions.

Listen to or read the extract. Note down ten vivid adjectives that Tanya and the interviewer use to describe her experiences.

....

.... [10]

b) Listen or read again and note down ten phrases that Tanya uses that relate to the senses.

....

....

.... **[10]**

Transcript: Extract from an interview

Interviewer: So, Tanya, you've just come back from an extraordinary trip: you've been swimming with sharks. Tell me, how did that come about?

Tanya: Well, I've always been fascinated by sharks. I first saw a real one when my parents took me to Scotland. We went on a boat ride and one leapt out of the water right in front of us. It was the most astonishing thing I'd ever seen! I felt terrified and shocked at first because the animal was enormous and I'd not expected to see it practically face to face. We got splashed quite badly. I could taste the salty water and my clothes were drenched and I started feeling numb with cold, but it didn't matter. After our holiday, I was still thrilled about it all and started trying to find out everything I could about sharks.

Interviewer: And you've done some charity work for sharks, is that right?

Tanya: Yes, that's right. Many shark species are endangered because of over-fishing and climate change, but we need sharks; they help get rid of weak and ill fish, which keeps fish populations healthy. So I help organise charity events where we raise awareness of the problem and collect money for conservation projects. One of the charities sponsored me to go swimming with sharks.

Interviewer: And what was that like?

Tanya: It was the most incredible experience. I got basic training but I did feel nervous. At first, I couldn't see anything and I could feel my heart beating in my chest. Then a shark appeared and it was both energising and peaceful. I've never felt more emotional in my whole life.

Total marks /40

Reading skills

You must be able to:

- understand and select information
- identify the overall viewpoint and understand the main points in a text
- see connections between ideas and make notes to summarise a text.

Understanding and selecting the main points

The main point of view in both written and spoken texts is the standpoint from which a person talks about a topic. It is either:

- for/in favour of/positive about/approving of an idea OR
- against/negative about/disapproving of an idea.

Seeing connections between ideas and making notes to summarise

If you have to write a summary, it is a good idea to make notes first. Remember, notes are not sentences; they are usually single words or phrases that give you the basic meaning and help you remember an idea. Notes should be short, they should be in your own words, and they should give information about the ideas in a text, e.g. different points of view.

Revision check

Words that go together

1. Cover the second column of the table. Which words complete these phrases from Chapter 8?

get away	with	less practice
learn something	by	heart
take pride	in	your culture
be addicted	to	gaming
soak	up	the atmosphere

Writing skills

You must be able to:

- use examples to support your point of view when writing
- use powerful language to make your opinions persuasive
- include opposite points of view to develop your own.

Using examples to support your point of view when writing

When you write or speak, you can support your opinion and be more convincing and persuasive by giving reasons and examples. An example can be either from your own experience or what you have seen or heard. Examples back up your opinion because:

- they provide evidence that something exists
- they show how/when/where something takes place.

Using powerful language to make your opinions persuasive

You can persuade people by describing things in a strong, positive way. For example, you could use 'spectacular' to describe fireworks rather than 'good', or 'wander' instead of 'walk slowly'.

Including opposite points of view to develop your own

You can be more persuasive by acknowledging another viewpoint and then trying to overcome this with your own arguments. You can use language such as 'but', 'however', 'while it is true that', 'to some extent it is true that', and 'in fact'.

> **Real life tip**
>
> Increase your vocabulary by noticing the language others use. Find powerful, interesting words by looking at the right types of texts, e.g. travel brochures, marketing leaflets or advertisements in English. Study them carefully and look for the words used to make us believe what is said about things.

Revision check

Words that go together

1. Cover the second column of the table. Which words from Chapter 8 go with the words in the first column?

breathtaking	landscape
ethnic	group
street	culture
ceremonial	ritual
mainstream	society

Words connected with festivals

2. Complete these words from Chapter 8.

> festiv_ _ _ _s
> proc _ _ _ion
> p_r_de
> f_ _ _w_ rks
> pag_ _ nt
> fl_ _t

Speaking skills

You must be able to:

- use examples to support your opinions while speaking
- include facts and expert opinions to support your point of view
- use rhetorical questions to make your speaking effective.

Using examples, facts and expert opinions to support your point of view

You can be more persuasive if you use examples to support your point of view. Examples often give reasons. It is also useful to add facts, especially those that are 'expert opinions', as they:

- show you have done some research
- give a better idea of exactly when, where and how something takes place.

To gather facts or evidence, you need to do research, e.g. on the internet or in the library.

Notice the difference between the following examples:

Many young people play computer games.	weak evidence
There is evidence that playing computer games for more than three hours a day makes people more likely to become addicted to gaming.	strong evidence

Using rhetorical questions to make your speaking effective

Good presentations often use rhetorical questions. They are asked for effect and do not require an answer. Instead, they prompt the audience to think. For example: *Obviously, computers are useful to us in many ways. But is usefulness the best way to measure the value of something?*

> **Revision check**

Words that go together

1. Cover the first column of the table. Which words from Chapter 8 go with the words in the second column?

learn	the basics
achieve	mastery
require	practice
release	a video
take	a tour
preserve	a culture

Art forms

2. Complete these words from Chapter 8.

c_ll_gr_phy
b_ll_t
c_rp_t w_ _v_ng
F_n_ _rts

Listening skills

You must be able to:

- understand and select relevant information in spoken texts
- identify and understand opinions in a range of spoken texts
- identify and understand conflicting opinions in an informal spoken text.

Understanding and selecting relevant information

There are many situations when you might hear a lot of information in a short space of time. You need to be able to find out quickly whether someone is giving you facts or opinions. If they give you facts, it is easier to trust them. Opinions are a person's beliefs or views; a fact can be proven but an opinion cannot.

You can work out whether someone is stating an opinion by listening to the language they use. The following phrases help identify opinions: 'It's normal/a shame/wonderful/terrible that ...'.

Also, watch out for words like 'never', 'always', 'better', 'best' and 'obviously'.

Identifying and understanding (conflicting) opinions

A conversation between two or more people is often more difficult to understand because different people are likely to hold different opinions about the same thing. When listening, you have to work out who holds which opinion.

> ### Real life tip
>
> Next time you and your friends have to make a decision, e.g. about where to go, and there is a discussion, listen carefully. How does each person try to persuade the others? Who gives evidence for their opinions? Noticing how people give opinions in your own language can help you do this in English.

Revision check

Verbs

1. Complete these words from Chapter 8.

```
evo_ _ _
_dm_re
dism_ _s
rej_ _t
r_v_ re _
```

Words that go together

2. Cover the second column of the table. Which words complete these phrases from Chapter 8?

a traditional way of	life
a higher dance	form
rich	heritage
a minority	language
an urban	lifestyle

1 **Read these definitions and write the words they define.**

a) the art of producing beautiful handwriting using a brush or a special pen ....

b) the craft or activity of making objects, such as pots and dishes out of clay, before baking them in an oven ....

c) a type of very skilled and artistic dancing with carefully planned movements ....

d) a form of popular culture which started among young black people in the United States in the 1980s and which includes rap music and graffiti art ....

e) the ideas, customs, and art of a particular society ....

[5]

2 **a)** Read the texts below. Underline the facts and circle the opinions.

Text 1

Hip hop and street dance might be popular at the local club but they shouldn't be welcomed as an art dance form at a national dance competition. There's far too much of it in competitions nowadays. Forms of dance, such as ballet and tap, have a long and creditable history and require hours and hours of practice to achieve high levels of technique and mastery. Hip hop does not require this level of practice and cannot be compared to these other higher dance forms. Hip hop's obsession with tricks like balancing on your head reduces dance to mere show. Dance should be about grace, beauty and culture.
There has been too much encouragement of hip hop, and dance schools and competitions like this one should be encouraging young people to learn the basics of dance through concentrating on classical dance.

Text 2

You obviously don't know what you're talking about! Street dance is just as valid as classical dance and they deserved to win. Two years ago I met a lot of hip hop dancers who all belonged to an underground street culture – all with superhuman strength and abilities. They could fly in the air. They could bend their elbows all the way back. They could spin on their heads 80 times in a row.
Our new dancers come from hip hop and street culture. Dance is changing and evolving and people need to realise that. Online videos and social networking between dancers have created a global laboratory online for dance. I've seen kids in Japan take moves from a YouTube video created in Detroit, copy them, change them within days, and release a new video. And this is happening every day. And from bedrooms and living rooms and garages, with cheap webcams, will come the world's great dancers of tomorrow. And because these dancers can now talk across different continents, hip hop will transform dance and change the world.

[24]

2 **b)** Read the texts again and find the following:

   1 one acknowledgment of a different point of view

   ....

   .... **[2]**

   2 one reason for an opinion.

   ....

   .... **[2]**

c) Read the texts again and find words that have the meanings below. They are in the same order as the texts.

Text 1: 1 need ....   2 get ....   3 just ....

Text 2: 4 great ....   5 turn ....   6 understand ....

       7 made ....   8 change .... **[8]**

3 Read the statements below. Then write rhetorical questions that could replace the statements in speeches.

a) I am going to talk about a number of reasons for this.

....

b) I can tell you why dance is a really important art form.

....

c) This problem can be solved in a number of ways.

....

d) I can tell you how often this happens.

....

e) We can ask ourselves if this is a good enough reason.

....

f) Dance schools should do something different instead.

.... **[6]**

....

                                                            Total marks   **/47**

Reading skills

You must be able to:

- identify and understand opinions in a range of texts
- recognise the language used to express opinion
- recognise and understand opinions which are implied but not directly stated.

Identifying and understanding opinions

When you read a text, it is important to be able to tell the difference between facts and the writer's opinion. Remember:

- a fact is something that can be proved, such as a date
- an opinion is what a person thinks or feels. It cannot be proved beyond doubt.

Writers sometimes use phrases such as 'in my opinion' and 'I think' to express their point of view, but not always. You will still need to recognise that a comment may just be personal opinion.

Writers often support a personal opinion with facts or reasons to convince their reader that their point of view is valid.

Recognising the language used to express opinion

In order to distinguish between fact and opinion you can do the following:

	How?	Language to look for
Identifying facts	Look for information that can be proved to be true.	dates, numbers
Identifying opinions	If something cannot be proved, it is probably opinion.	phrases such as 'in my opinion', 'I think that'

Recognising and understanding opinions which are implied

Adjectives (e.g. 'a **great** journey') can be used to signal an opinion about what someone has seen or experienced. They add more information to a factual account and give the reader an idea of how the writer feels, without them having to say it directly.

Revision check

Words that go together

1. Cover the second column of the table. Which words complete these phrases from Chapter 9?

go	on	a journey
travel	for	leisure
go	by	boat
travel	at	speed
travel	for	pleasure

Noun phrases

2. Complete these words from Chapter 9.

```
_ir tr_v_l
b_s serv_ _ _
tr_n_p_rt s_st_m
in_ _ _-city r_ _ _way
st_ _m l_c_m_t_ve
co_ _unic_tions sat_llit_
```

Writing skills

You must be able to:

- use relative pronouns to join sentences
- use a variety of structures when writing descriptions
- join your ideas and sentences using connectives (connecting words and phrases).

Using relative pronouns to join sentences

When you write, you can use a variety of sentence structures to join your ideas together. You have already learned about ways to combine simple sentences to make compound and complex sentences (see Chapter 3), but you can also use relative pronouns.

Relative pronouns

Relative pronoun	Function	Example
who	introduces information about people	Mr Moss was the teacher **who** encouraged me most at school.
that/which	introduces information about things	These are the trainers **that** everyone wants at the moment.
where	introduces information about places	This is the park **where** we like to play.

Using a variety of structures when writing descriptions

When you describe something, try to use a range of structures to add interest to your writing.

You can do this by using:

- sentences of different lengths
- different types of sentences (simple, compound and complex)
- adjectives
- noun phrases (see Chapter 3)
- relative pronouns.

Joining ideas and sentences using connectives

Complex sentences can express more sophisticated ideas, for example to compare or to add information.

Connectives	Use
even though	to contrast to show that something happens despite a problem or difficulty
because	to show cause and effect to give a reason or reasons why something happens
although	to contrast – similar to 'even though' – introduces a statement which makes the main statement seem surprising
when	to add further information about an event

Speaking skills

You must be able to:

- use a variety of grammatical structures accurately and effectively when you speak
- vary the tense of verbs you use according to the situation.

Using a variety of grammatical structures

You can use modals to express your arguments and opinions in a more sophisticated way. These words show subtle shades of meaning, such as ability, possibility, obligation or necessity.

Example	Function
I can walk.	ability
I could walk.	possibility
I ought to walk.	the right thing to do
I should walk.	the right thing to do
I must walk.	obligation

Master simple modals, e.g. 'can', 'must' and 'should' before using them in the past tense and other more complex forms.

Varying the tense of verbs you use according to the situation

When you are speaking, it is important to express yourself clearly and fluently. This includes using the correct verb tense in the correct situation.

Example	Time	Tense
I ride my bike to college.	the present	present tense
I walked to school when I was younger.	the past	past tense
It used to be quite quick, but now it's really slow.	the past	past tense ('used to' to compare the past and the present)
When I'm older, I'll drive to work.	the future	future tense

Revision check

Words that go together

1. Cover the first column of the table. Which words complete these phrases from Chapter 9?

set	off on a journey
let	off steam
dig	up the countryside
release	dangerous gases
catch	a ferry

Nouns

2. Complete these words from Chapter 9.

co_g_ _tion
spacecr_ _ _
inf_ast_ _cture
p_ _estria_
l_ _nch pad
pet_ _l

Listening skills

You must be able to:

- understand connections and differences between related ideas to answer multiple-choice questions
- understand what is implied but not directly stated in a formal spoken text.

Understanding connections and differences between related ideas

When you answer multiple-choice questions about listening texts, first read the questions and underline any key words to help you listen out for the answers. If, the first time you listen, you are not sure which is the right answer, put question marks in pencil by the possible answers and then listen again before deciding on the right answer.

Understanding what is implied in a formal spoken text

When we talk to one another we do not always 'spell out' exactly what we mean. In the same way, when you listen to someone, you have to be ready to understand what they imply but not state directly. Try to think of different ways in which the information you are listening out for could be expressed; you may not hear it in the form you expect.

> **Real life tip**
>
> To prepare yourself for listening to information that is not directly stated, practise saying things in different ways. You can make this into a game. With your friends, take it in turns to repeat what somebody has said in a different way. If you can't think of anything, you are 'out'; the last person to come up with an answer wins.

> **Revision check**
>
> **Words that go together**
>
> 1. Cover the first column of the table. Which words complete these phrases from Chapter 9?

carry	passengers
exceed	my expectations
be	unheard of
run	on coal
overlook	the sea

1 **Match the words 1–7 with the words a–g.**

1 mass	a) flight
2 intercity	b) seat
3 bus	c) transport
4 steam	d) pad
5 space	e) locomotive
6 launch	f) railway
7 comfy	g) service

[7]

2 **Read the four statements in each set. Tick the one that has a very different meaning to the other three.**

a) 1 Cats like the outdoors. ☐

2 Cats are animals that like to be in the wild. ☐

3 Cats need a lot of exercise. ☐

4 It is best not to keep cats locked up in the house. ☐

b) 1 According to official guidelines, we should do up to 1.5 hours of exercise a week. ☐

2 Three half-hours of exercise are sufficient in any seven-day period, if you cannot do more. ☐

3 Doctors agree that 90 minutes of exercise a week is the minimum we should be doing. ☐

4 Professionals recommend 90 minutes of exercise a week or more. ☐

c) 1 More and more people in cities are finding public transport convenient. ☐

2 Statistics show that public transport is becoming more popular in cities. ☐

3 The use of personal vehicles to get about in cities is on the decline. ☐

4 Buses and trains are being used more frequently in rural locations these days. ☐ [6]

3 **Complete the text with the correct tense of the verbs in brackets.** [8]

I think there (a) .... (be) lots of problems with transport today. For example, many people in my town (b) .... (drive) to work every day. We (c) .... (have) a good train service here, which (d) .... (go) straight to the city centre. However, train tickets nowadays are lot more expensive than they (e) .... (be). They are too expensive for most people to use every day. But petrol also (f) .... (cost) a lot and I think it (g) .... (get) more expensive in the future. In my opinion, there should be a better bus service. Buses are cheap, practical and they (h) .... (not cause) as much pollution as cars.

4 **Complete the text with the words in the box.**

| because | can | even though | should | that | when | where | who |

[8]

‹ travel blog

HOME   ABOUT   SKILLS   CONTACT   **BLOG**

Hello, readers!

This is the third update about my new life in the UK. I hope you're still enjoying this blog!

I've now been in London for four months and I've finally found a place (a) .... I think I might stay for longer than a few weeks. It's a flat in Stoke Newington and (b) .... it's tiny, it's in a lovely area, so I don't mind. I hope not to spend too much time at home anyway! When you're in a busy city, I think you (c) .... really try to go out, enjoy it and take part in activities (d) .... are cultural or fun – or both – whenever you (e) ....

Talking of things I've been doing, in my last blog post I mentioned a friend (f) .... works in the head office of a chain of restaurants, and I've been going along with her to launch parties. I'm not saying this to make you all jealous (although you should be; there was free food ☺!), but (g) .... you'll be hearing a lot more about her in my next post, (h) .... I tell you about the crazy week I've just had. You're just going to have to wait until then, though; it's time for me to go to work!

Anna

5 **List the following as fast as you can:**

a) four nouns that can go with the word 'space'

.... [4]

b) three relative pronouns

.... [3]

c) two phrases that have a similar meaning to 'travel'

.... [2]

d) three adjectives that can be used to describe a landscape

.... [3]

e) three connectives.

.... [3]

Total marks /44

Reading skills

You must be able to:

- find facts and details from complex texts that present information in different forms
- understand and use information presented in different forms.

Finding and understanding facts and details from maps, diagrams and timelines

Reading information presented in different forms is a key skill for understanding complex texts. Processes may be described using diagrams, maps or flow charts. Timelines can also be used to clarify meaning.

To find detailed information in texts with visuals like maps, diagrams and timelines:

- Read for detail. Look at the text and understand how it fits with the diagram.
- Look for labels, arrows, small print or shaded parts that explain the diagram.
- Notice dates and arrows in a timeline. See how they relate to one another.
- Look for the key on a map. It might colour code countries, cities, seas, etc.

Real life tip

Do not ignore visual information. Get into the habit of studying visuals. For example, if you are given an advertising leaflet, try to work out what the company wants you to know just by looking at any diagrams. If there is text as well, check if it gives any extra information – it is possible that you could work everything out from the visuals alone.

Revision check

Words connected with silk

1. Complete these words from Chapter 10.

b_ _e of si_ _
f_ _r_c
_oom
silkw_ _ _
spi_ a coc_ _ _
th_ _ _d
tr_d_ r_ _te
eav _ilk

Writing skills

You must be able to:

- use a range of appropriate vocabulary effectively in your writing
- use comparatives and superlatives correctly
- use formal and informal vocabulary appropriately.

Using a range of appropriate vocabulary effectively

Building a wide and varied vocabulary is the key to sounding like an expert. When you come across new vocabulary, try the following:

- Guess what the word means from its context.
- Identify the form of the word – is it a noun, verb, adjective or adverb?
- Look for picture clues that might tell you what the word means.
- Look out for metaphors or similes using 'like' or 'as'.

Using comparatives and superlatives correctly

You can compare ideas or thoughts by using comparative or superlative adjectives.

Type	Meaning	Formation	Example	Exceptions
comparative	*more* or *less*	• add *-er* • add *more*	• *short – shorter* • *beautiful – more beautiful*	*good – better* *bad – worse*
superlative	*most*	• add *the* and *-est* • add *the most*	• *short – the shortest* • *beautiful – the most beautiful*	*good – the best* *bad – the worst*

Using formal and informal vocabulary appropriately

It is important to choose words that give your writing the right tone. This will depend on why you are writing, and for whom. A formal piece of writing demands formal vocabulary. In informal writing, e.g. a blog, you might write 'Check out …'; in formal writing you would say 'Look carefully at …'.

> ## Revision check
>
> **Nouns and noun phrases**
>
> 1. Put the words in the correct column.
>
> | bandana |
> | bell-bottom trousers |
> | beret   cowboy boots |
> | denim jacket   flats |
> | graduation cap |
> | ripped jeans   sandals |
>
> | On your feet | On your head | On your body |
> |---|---|---|
> | | | |
> | | | |
> | | | |

Speaking skills

You must be able to:

- use exactly the right words when speaking about culture and clothing
- use more specialised vocabulary appropriately.

Using exactly the right words

To talk effectively about a particular topic, you need to develop your knowledge of some specific and detailed vocabulary. You should therefore categorise groups of similar words.

Here are some examples of useful vocabulary related to the topic of clothing and culture:

Headwear	Adjectives that describe styles of clothing
turbans bowler hats helmets headscarves veils	flared (e.g. trousers) baggy (e.g. shirt) fitted (e.g. jacket) low-slung (e.g. jeans) tight-fitting (e.g. jeans)

Real life tip

Your vocabulary notebook can be an online file if you like. When you are learning words that can be illustrated, e.g. fashion-related words, it is useful to put pictures next to the new vocabulary rather than explanations or translations.

Using more specialised vocabulary appropriately

Using vocabulary accurately and sensitively to communicate your ideas is a key skill. The wider your vocabulary, the better you will be able to express exactly what you mean.

Revision check

Words that go together

1. Cover the second column of the table. Which words complete these phrases from Chapter 10?

a splash of	colour
a vibrant	colour
a flexible	dress code
a must-have	outfit
high-waisted	trousers

Adjectives to describe styles

2. Complete these words from Chapter 10.

cl_ _ _ic
dist_ _ _tive
_xt_em_
in_ovat_ _ _
tim_l_ _ _
v_ rs_t_le

Listening skills

You must be able to:

- listen effectively to fellow students
- understand and select detailed information supplied by fellow students
- understand what is implied but not directly stated in a conversation.

Listening effectively and understanding and selecting detailed information

To communicate effectively, you need to:

- listen attentively
- ask people to explain things in more detail when you are unsure what you have heard
- listen carefully to the questions people ask you
- respond and make use of as wide a vocabulary as possible.

Understanding what is implied in a conversation

Good listeners understand what other people are implying. This is especially important when you are listening to people who have different points of view. You need to pay attention to the tone they use, their body language, their spoken language and their choice of words.

> **Real life tip**
>
> It can be difficult to understand people speaking in a different language to your own; natural speech can sound fast, so it is difficult to distinguish the separate words. However, the more you listen, the easier it gets. You will get better at listening by becoming familiar with a variety of British and other native English speakers accents.

> **Revision check**
>
> **Words that go together**
>
> 1. Cover the second column of the table. Which words from Chapter 10 go with the words in the first column?
>
> | precious | stone |
> |----------|-------|
> | track | pants |
> | martial | arts |
> | fur | trade |
> | unfair | wages |
>
> **Nouns**
>
> 2. Complete these words from Chapter 10.
>
> | Jobs | Materials | Animals |
> |------|-----------|---------|
> | t_ _l_ r | l_ce | f_x |
> | cr_ftsm_n | l_ _th_r | _tt_r |
> | _mbr_ _d_rer | n_lon | r_c_ _ _n dog |

1 **Look at the flow chart. Then read the text below.**

a) Underline three places in the text that give different information from the flow chart. [3]

b) Highlight information that is in the text but not in the flow chart. [4]

'Fashion for all' – How to apply

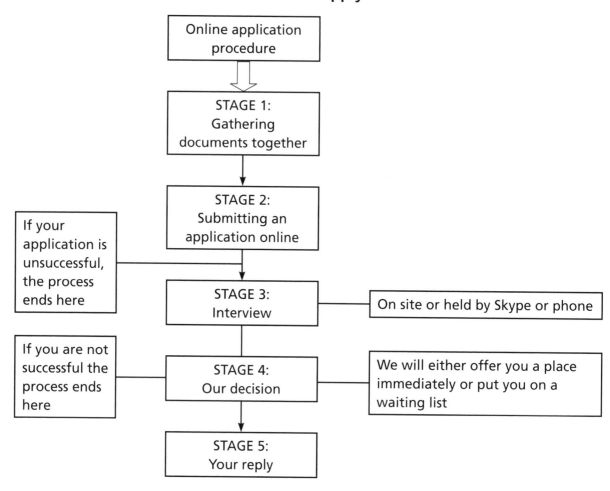

If you would like to apply online for our 'Fashion for beginners' course, you will need to follow a six-step process. First of all, you will need to gather all your documents. Please refer to the checklist on the next page to make sure you have them all. You will need to scan these. Then go to the application web page, click here, to fill in a short form and submit your scanned documents. All applicants will be granted an interview, face to face or by Skype or phone. There are three possible outcomes: successful, unsuccessful, or you will be placed on a waiting list. If you are offered a place, you will need to let us know in writing, within two weeks, whether you accept the offer or not.

2 Match the statements 1–7 with the requests for clarification a–g.

1 Our course lasts two years, but it's followed by a five-month placement in the fashion industry.	a) I'm not sure where you said it takes place?
2 In your second year you will learn about different hat designs, from berets to turbans.	b) Could you give me a little more detail about what happens in the show, please?
3 There are different ways of getting involved in the fashion show, both behind the scenes and on stage.	c) Could you tell me again what you said about passing the course?
4 We usually hold the show at the college, but sometimes we use spaces at factories and offices.	d) Could you repeat what you said about the duration of the course, please?
5 In the first year, we have 80 students on the course, but they all have different interests, so they take a variety of classes and there are usually no more than 20 in a group.	e) Sorry, when you were talking about designs, did you say 'bandanas'?
6 To be successful, you'll need to get more than 50 per cent in all your exams and your practical work.	f) You mentioned 'fluro'; could you clarify what you mean by that?
7 Students work with different materials like silk or cotton, they experiment with colour; they might use fluro, for example, and they use different types of cuts.	g) How many did you say there were in total?

[7]

3 Complete the sentences with the comparative or superlative form of the adjectives in brackets.

a) We believe we have .... (good) course in London.

b) Our students are .... (hard) and .... (talented) workers.

c) Our students take part in a .... (large) number of shows than those of most other colleges.

d) Studying here will be .... (great) opportunity you will ever have.

e) We are .... (old) college in the city.

f) You could not find .... (supportive) or .... (kind) teachers anywhere.

g) You could not find a .... (good) place to study.

[9]

Total marks   /23

Reading skills

You must be able to:

- understand and select relevant information
- identify points for and against a point of view in a text
- recognise a point of view when it is implied and not directly stated.

Understanding and selecting relevant information

Article writers often build a balanced argument by giving reasons for and against an issue. You should:

- identify the reasons
- decide if the writer is for or against the issue
- decide whether the reasons given are valid.

Identifying points for and against a point of view

To introduce a reason to support or to oppose an argument, writers often use phrases such as:

Supporting	Opposing
On the one hand, … Moreover, … Furthermore, … Firstly, … Secondly, … Since In view of the fact that …	On the other hand, … In contrast, … However, …

Recognising a point of view when it is implied

You need to be able to work out someone's opinion when it is not stated directly. For example:

*The band strutted on stage but **only** managed to sing three songs.*	Negative opinion: The word 'only' implies that singing three songs is not enough.
*The band strutted on stage and **wowed** the audience from the first minute with the **stunning** power of their guitar playing.*	Positive opinion: The words 'wowed' and 'stunning' are strong, positive words.

Revision check

Words that go together

1. Cover the second column of the table. Which words from Chapter 11 go with the words in the first column?

a piece of	classical music
the music	industry
copyright	law
a criminal	act
a contentious	issue
band	practice

Writing skills

You must be able to:

- punctuate speech correctly
- use a wide range of punctuation correctly and effectively.

Punctuating speech correctly

Remember:

- quotation marks around someone's words: *'I prefer non-fiction,' said Lara*.
- when spoken words come first: a comma or question mark inside the quotation marks after the last word spoken: *'What happened?' she asked*.
- when spoken words come last: speaker's first word has a capital letter; comma before the first quotation mark: *She asked, 'What kind of things do you read?'*
- when a new person starts speaking, start a new line.

Using a wide range of punctuation correctly and effectively

Punctuation and spelling mistakes make writing difficult to read. You need to use a range of punctuation marks.

Punctuation mark	Purpose	Example
apostrophe	for omission	*We're [are] reading a book.*
	for possession	*The girl's writing is neat.* (the writing of one girl) *The girls' writing is neat.* (the writing of all the girls)
colon	to introduce a list	*I like the following types of entertainment: TV, film, and music.*
	to introduce words in a dialogue/ interview	*Reporter: What do you usually write? Author: Adventure or mystery stories.*
pairs of commas	to add non-essential details	*Her father, who is retired, spends hours reading newspapers.*
brackets (also called **parentheses**)	to set information apart	*The journalist wrote articles (more than four a day) at an astonishing rate.*

Revision check

Words connected with genres of literature

1. Complete these words from Chapter 11.

gra_ _ _ _   nov_ _
ro_ _ _ce
_ _ _iller
non- f_ _ _ _ _n
d_ _ma
sc_ _ _ _e fi_ _ _ _ _
his_ _ _ _ _al _ _ _ _ion
p_ _ _ry
_ _rror

Words that go together

2. Cover the first column of the table. Which words complete these phrases from Chapter 11?

build up	a fan base
download	a song
take part	in an orchestra
wow	an audience
produce	music

Speaking skills

You must be able to:

- disagree politely in a conversation
- keep a conversation going by rephrasing what the previous speaker has said.

Disagreeing politely in a conversation

When disagreeing, try not to simply say 'no'; people might think you are being impolite. There are better ways to disagree. There are many phrases you can use to disagree politely or to introduce your own idea. For example:

- I take your point, but that's not the way I see it.
- Perhaps, but I can't help thinking that …
- No thank you. I'd rather not.
- I see what you mean, but I'm not convinced that …
- I'm not sure about that; however, what about …

Keeping a conversation going

Here are some ways to keep a conversation going. Note especially what Speaker 2 says:

	Speaker 1	Speaker 2
Listen carefully and then ask questions to find out more.	*English was my best class today.*	*Really? What did you do?*
Agree and then give your opinion.	*I read a lot more non-fiction than fiction.*	*Oh yes, we read a lot of non-fiction in school.*
Rephrase to show you have understood.	*I can't afford to get satellite TV.*	*Mm, yes. The monthly subscription is expensive.*

> **Real life tip**
>
> Listen to conversations in your own language, particularly when you know people have different opinions, e.g. about sports or TV programmes. Do your friends disagree with each other differently from the way adults disagree? Is there a difference in approach and in the language they use?

> **Revision check**
>
> **Types of TV programmes**
>
> 1. Complete these words from Chapter 11.
>
> d_ _ce progr_ _ _ _
> f_ _tb_ _ _ high_ _ _ _ _s
> c_arts pr_ _ _amme
> c_at sho_
> do_ _ _ _ _ _ary
> nat_ _ _l _ _ _tory p_ _ _ _ _mme
> f_ _m
> the n_ _s
> soap o_ _ _ _

Listening skills

You must be able to:

- understand and select facts in both formal and informal spoken texts
- recognise and understand opinions and attitudes in a more formal dialogue.

Understanding and selecting facts

Most texts mix fact and opinion. It is important to be able to tell facts from opinions so that you can decide for yourself whether you believe something or someone.

Remember:

Fact	something you can prove to be true
Opinion	what someone thinks or feels about a subject and cannot be proved

Recognising and understanding opinions and attitudes

Sometimes one word, e.g. an adjective, can change a fact into an opinion. Look at the difference in these examples:

fact: *It's got fight scenes.*

opinion: *It's got **thrilling** fight scenes.*

Real life tip

Make sure you get used to listening to a variety of texts. You might like listening to English language radio programmes about music, but you could also listen to factual programmes, e.g. about current affairs. Try to include programmes that feature informal discussions, e.g. a chat show, as well as formal discussions, e.g. experts discussing medical developments.

Revision check

Words that go together

1. Cover the first column of the table. Which words complete these phrases from Chapter 11?

a star-	studded film
a slow-	moving film
a jaw-	dropping scene
an action-	packed film
a nerve-	wracking ending
a laugh-out-	loud performance
an all-singing,	all-dancing movie

2. Cover the first column of the table. Which words complete these phrases from Chapter 11?

shoot	a film
keep	people informed
catch	up on the news
be	in favour of file-sharing
amuse	yourself

1 **List the following as fast as you can:**

a) five adjectives that you can use to express what you think about a film scene

....

[5]

b) four types of fiction

....

[4]

c) six types of TV programmes.

....

[6]

2 a) 🎧 **11** This task can be done by listening to the extract from a school discussion online, or reading the transcript of the audio below. If you listen to the audio, cover the transcript and then answer the questions.

Listen to or read the extract and note down the language used to keep the conversation going.

Method	Language used to keep the conversation going
Listening carefully and then asking questions to find out more.	1 ....
Agreeing and then giving your opinion.	2 .... 3 .... 4 ....
Rephrasing to show you have understood.	5 ....

[5]

> **Transcript: Extract from a school discussion**
>
> **Kate:** Thank you all for being here. Today's topic is e-readers, and we will be discussing what is better, a book or an e-reader. As I'm sure we all know, an e-reader is a portable device that allows users to download and read texts in electronic form. They became popular in this country about 10 years ago and many people are now using them to read books, er...
>
> **Josh:** Sorry, Kate, but I was wondering if you know what the numbers are – how many people are using them?
>
> **Kate:** Thanks for your question, Josh. I don't have the exact numbers, but I think I've read somewhere that in the US alone over 80 million people use the devices. So they're clearly very popular and people are able to see the benefits. I thought we could start by talking about the advantages.

Hannah:	That's a good idea, but I think I'd like to start by talking about the advantages of *books*.
Kate:	Yes, of course, we can talk about those, and we can compare the benefits of both.
Hannah:	Well, for me, books are physical. I like to touch, feel and smell them.
Josh:	Yes, they're something you can hold, and then you can keep them and put them in a bookcase and be reminded of them and their stories.
Kate:	I see what you're saying but you need space for that, and an advantage of an e-reader is that you can have lots of books without having to move house!
Hannah:	Perhaps, but I can always find some more space for my favourites.
Kate:	I take your point, Hannah, but when I go on holiday I find it much easier to take five e-books in my handbag rather than fill my suitcase with books.
Josh:	Yes, when you're travelling, it's better to take something light. I have to say that that's the only advantage for me, though. I still prefer books all other times.
Kate:	I'm not sure that's the only advantage. They allow us to read in the dark, to look up words instantly, and to make the letters bigger if our eyesight is not so good.
Hannah:	Yes, they're great for disabled people and they have more functions, but for me a printed book is more than enough to keep me happy.

b) Listen or read again and note down the language used to disagree.

1 ....

2 ....

3 ....

4 ....

5 ....   [5]

3 Punctuate the text from a school magazine below. Add two quotation marks, two pairs of commas, one colon and two apostrophes.

On Friday 12 October, we held several class discussions about a variety of topics. As I am really interested in literature, I have chosen to write about the group that discussed the topic of e-readers. There were three participants in this group Kate, Josh and Hannah. Kate who had been chosen to lead the debate started by thanking the audience and by defining e-readers. In the discussion, Kate seemed to prefer e-readers, but Josh said, I still prefer books, even though he agreed they were useful when travelling. Hannah the third group member admitted that e-readers were functional and useful but personally, she preferred books as they were physical. I cant tell you who won the argument on the day, but I can say that it was very interesting for everyone concerned and that the participants contributions were highly valued by the audience.

[9]

Total marks   /34

Reading skills

You must be able to:

- recognise both facts and opinions in different types and lengths of text
- understand how the use of language may suggest a viewpoint.

Recognising both facts and opinions

When you read a formal text, you need to be able to tell the difference between facts and opinions, and also to identify the author's viewpoint.

Articles in newspapers, magazines and on websites are often a writer's viewpoint – the main belief they want to convey – and they will use facts and other opinions to present it. You need to realise that they have researched the topic and formed a viewpoint based on what they have discovered.

Understanding how the use of language may suggest a viewpoint

The adjectives a writer uses can give you a strong impression of their opinion. Nouns and verbs can also tell us about their attitude; they can suggest or imply an attitude.

Part of speech	Example	Implied meaning
adjective	*spectacular* scenery	the writer loves the scenery: positive
noun	a *crowd* of people	a large group of people: neutral
	a *mob* of people	a large, disorganised, perhaps violent, group of people: negative
verb	The man *swaggered* up to the bar.	to walk or behave arrogantly: negative
	We *ambled* back to the car.	to walk at a leisurely relaxed pace: neutral

Revision check

Words that go together

1. Cover the second column of the table. Which words complete these phrases from Chapter 12?

lower the voting age	to	16
have more	at	stake
engage	with	a topic
be	in	your twenties
be new	to	blogging
have access	to	education

Stages of life

2. Complete these words from Chapter 12.

in_ _ncy
ad_ _esc_ _ce
y_ _th
adult_ _ _ _
old _ _ _

Writing skills

You must be able to:

- choose the correct tone and style for different readers and different situations.

Choosing the correct tone and style

You always need to think about the purpose of your writing. You need to use the correct tone and style to suit your reader. If you are writing to your employer, for example, you need to use formal language; in an informal situation you will use a different vocabulary and different sentence structures.

Always think about who your text is for. A text for young people may need short sentences with simple words and little or no technical language. It might also be important to make it fun and interesting. An older reader would prefer more sophisticated language and a variety of sentence types.

Here are some differences between formal and informal writing:

Type of writing	Type of language	Example
Formal (e.g. a letter to/ from a teacher)	formal language to start	*Dear Madam, Thank you for ...*
	full forms	*I have written a letter to your parents ...*
	avoid using idioms	*The weather was extremely hot.*
	formal language to end	*Yours faithfully*
Informal writing (e.g. an email to a friend)	friendly, conversational start	*Hi, Thanks a million for ...*
	contracted forms	*I've written a letter to your mum and dad ...*
	use idioms	*It was boiling hot today.*
	friendly language to end	*Cheers!*

Speaking skills

You must be able to:

- speak clearly and use the correct stress when speaking
- vary your tone to interest your listener.

Speaking clearly and using the correct stress when speaking

When you want to tell a story or interest your listener, there are different techniques to make your speech more exciting or to convey your emotions more clearly. For example, you can:

- emphasise particular words and use a wide range of expression
- pause before some words to build up greater dramatic expression
- repeat certain words or vary the volume of your voice.

Remember: it is not just *what* you *say*, but *how* you say it that conveys an idea.

Varying your tone to interest your listener

You need to vary your tone to engage your listeners and keep them interested. This is true in both informal situations, e.g. when you tell a story to friends, or formal situations, e.g. when you give a presentation – an important and useful life skill – to a large group of people.

Real life tip

Think about interesting speakers and boring speakers, e.g. celebrities, presenters or people you know in real life. Next time you listen to them, work out why you think this about them. Do they emphasise certain words, pause occasionally, vary their pace, vary their volume – or not? Reflecting on other people's speech can make us more aware of our own, which is the first step toward improving it.

Revision check

Words that go together

1. Cover the second column of the table. Which words complete these phrases from Chapter 12?

coming-of-age	ceremony
minimum voting	age
job	creation
respectable member of	society
younger	generation

Listening skills

You must be able to:

- recognise and understand ideas, opinions and attitudes
- recognise connections between ideas
- understand what is implied but not directly stated.

Recognising and understanding ideas, opinions and attitudes

When you are listening, you may have to pick out specific information to answer questions or follow instructions. Think about what you need to find out before you listen. This will help you recognise and understand the ideas, opinions and attitudes that you hear.

Recognising connections between ideas

In longer listening texts, it can be more difficult to follow the main ideas and to understand how they are connected. Think about relevant words you should listen for. Also think of synonyms for these words as the text may use these instead. Doing this will help you focus on what you hear and enable you to answer the questions successfully.

Understanding what is implied

Sometimes the answers are not directly stated in the text. You need to work them out based on your understanding of the information you do hear.

Revision check

Words that go together

1. Cover the first column of the table. Which words complete these phrases from Chapter 12?

get	older
live	to be 100
move	out
pay	taxes
teach	an old dog new tricks

Nouns

1. Complete these words from Chapter 12.

```
mar_ _age
gover_ _ _ _t
i_ol_tion
_ _adequac_
per_ _ _tage
```

Chapter Test: Young and old

1 **Complete the phrases with the verbs in the box.**

become	get	leave	live	save up	shape	start	treat

a) .... an adult

b) .... to be 100

c) .... old

d) .... your own future

e) .... home

f) .... someone as an adult

g) .... money

h) .... a family

[8]

2 **Read the statements below. Then rewrite them using informal language.**

a) He is employed as an architect in a large firm.

....

b) I estimate that my great-grandmother is now in her nineties.

....

c) Joe suffered from asthma in his infancy.

....

d) Scientists rarely work in isolation; they usually collaborate with colleagues.

....

e) The price of televisions has decreased sharply.

....

f) Mr Barrett is web-illiterate.

....

[6]

3 a) The text on page 83 is a transcript of an interview on a website. Read Rita's answers out loud. Then record yourself reading them.

b) If possible, listen to the recording of the interview. Indicate in the text where Rita uses the following techniques:

1 emphasises words

2 pauses before certain words

3 varies the volume.

If you cannot listen to the recording, guess where she would do this.

c) Record yourself again, making sure you use the three techniques in 3b in the appropriate places.

Transcript: Extract from an interview

Interviewer: **Could you tell me a bit more about the 'Being-a-Friend' organisation?**

Rita: Well, Being-a-Friend brings people from all ages and walks of life together. People contact the organisation if they feel they'd like to have more people in their lives, and volunteers go and befriend them. We mainly work in cities, but people from all over the country can access the service.

Interviewer: **And what's your role?**

Rita: I'm one of the volunteers working with the elderly in Manchester. At the moment, I regularly visit three people, all over the age of 70, in their homes.

Interviewer: **And what do you do for these people?**

Rita: I don't do much, really. Sometimes something practical needs to be done, and I might do some shopping for them … but my main role is to spend time with them, listen to them, just be a good friend.

Interviewer: **What do you think about the work that 'Being-a-Friend' does?**

Rita: I think it's very important. I've only been with the organisation for two years, but in that time I've realised that many of the people I've visited don't see anybody else all week – just me. If the organisation wasn't there for them, they'd be very lonely. It's easy to get isolated. Very often, relatives move out or away, and people are left on their own. They don't like to cook just for themselves and they might not have friends who live nearby. It's what happens in cities. And then soon, they stop taking proper care of themselves. They stop being active altogether. That can have a negative impact on their health and how they feel about life. So having a friend from the organisation visit them can make a big difference to what they get out of life.

Interviewer: **And that's why you volunteer? To make people's lives better?**

Rita: Yes and no. Of course, it's lovely if people tell you they've had a great day or that they've really enjoyed an activity we did together. We often go to the shops, visit a garden centre, have a cup of tea … But that's not the only reason I do it. These people have had lives, they've had jobs, and they've had families. There have been amazing changes over their lifetimes. They have lots of interesting stories to tell. I like listening to people telling me about how different their lives used to be, and I always ask them what their opinions are about the way we do things now. I learn so much from them.

Interviewer: **Any final thoughts?**

Rita: Erm, I'm not sure … Yes. There is something. I just want to say that I want to be like that, you know? I'm nearly 18 now, but when I'm as old as these friends, I want to be just like them: full of interesting stories and happy to give advice to younger people.

Interviewer: **Thank you for your time.**

Rita: You're welcome!

Total marks   /14

Vocabulary: Chapter 1 – Technology

Internet

attitude to internet use
be online
cloud
Internet of Things (IoT)
linked pages
net
network
search engine
World Wide Web
Uniform Resource Locator (URL)
web
web browser
web surfing
website address

Communication

collaboration
contact
email
keep in touch
online chat
send/receive a text message
social networking
(traditional) method of
communication

Disadvantages of technology

absorb
brain damage
bring about a change
bully
cheat
confidential data
crash
discipline problem
distraction
disturbance
emit
focus concentration (on)
have an adverse effect (on)
health hazard
IT disaster
personal information
potential risk
prevent somebody from sleeping

radiation
spam email
status symbol
virus

Uses for technology

access
back up files
backup/automatic backup
benefit to teaching
calendar
cloud storage
demonstrate
entertain
file sharing
file transfer
memo
mobile banking
perform a basic task
reminder
research
storage
sync files
synchronise
tool
word processing

Products

android
application
cassette
cassette player
cellphone/mobile phone
driverless car
electronic system
e-portfolio
free trial
handheld device
mouse
(personal) computer
personal digital assistant (PDA)
smartphone
tablet
TV set
user guide
video equipment

Technical terms

byte
computing
data
digital
electronics
FTP client
GB (gigabyte)
hi-tech
integrated circuit
liquid crystal display
password
patent
storage capacity
technical wizard
upload
up-to-date

Advantages of technology

benefit
convenient
improvement
relevant
remarkable

Evolution of technology

coin a term
evolution of technology
inventor
technological invention
unwieldy

Discovering places

distant land
discovery
fleet
explorer
face danger
journey
landscape
map
quest
region
set off (on an expedition)
territory
trade
travels
trip
unexplored
voyage

Reasons for and against exploration

acquire
benefits to mankind
medical application
monitor (other countries' army and defence capabilities)
prepare for danger
see the world
spend (on)
the way forward

Space

astronaut
cabin
gaze at the stars
life on Mars
mission
satellite technology
space agency
space capsule
space programme
unmanned mission

Oil

explosion
gas flare
generate electricity
offshore/onshore
oil drilling
oil leak
oil reserves
oil rig/well
oil spill
petrol
poisonous fumes

At sea

armada
crew
deep sea/underwater exploration
ice cutter
junk
patrol boat
pirate
port
sailor
scuba diving
shipwreck
(two-berth) cabin
warship

Objects and history

Chinese Ming dynasty
civilisation
emperor
imperial court
ivory
laquerware
pearl
porcelain
silk
spice

The environment

deforestation
energy consumption
environmental impact
mineral deposits
off the (north) coast (of)
pole
renewable energy
solar/wind energy
species
surrounding area

Adjectives

accessible
ambitious
arctic
azure
divine
equipped (with)
glamorous
hazardous
illegal
inspire
mesmerising
once-in-a-lifetime
remote
well-heated

Verbs

be in awe (of)
crease
declared something a success
depend (on)
dream about/of
flatten
fold
research

Health, illness and disease

active/healthy lifestyle
be/stay healthy
diabetes
face an uphill battle
fatigue
give a new lease of life
have access to clean water/
healthcare/treatment
(malaria) vaccine
obese
obesity
overweight
poor health
save lives
slow the effects of ageing
weakness

Diet

balanced diet
be a vegetarian
calories
carbohydrate/carbs
dairy
deprive (the brain) of vital
nutrients
fats and oils
fizzy drink
follow a diet
junk food
low-fat
mineral
nutrient
nutrition
nutritional/vitamin supplement
organic food
protein
serving (of)
use something sparingly
vitamin (D/B12)

Cooking

boil/bring to the boil
brown
bunch (of coriander)
chop/chopped
chunk (of ginger)
clove (of garlic)
cook until tender
crush/crushed
flavour
fry
gram/g
ground (coriander)
ingredient
kilogram/kg
lower/reduce the heat
millilitre (ml)
season (to taste)
serve (with)
simmer
sprinkling (of coriander)
tablespoon/tbs (of)
teaspoon/tsp (of)

Food

basil
dry beans
filling
flavoured with
food group
fortified cereal
nuts
(olive) oil
poultry
raisins
saffron
yogurt

Activities

athletics (track)
break/set a world record
do exercise/karate/Pilates/yoga
go rock climbing/running/skiing/
swimming
play basketball/ice hockey
record a personal best
run a marathon
train (three times a week)

Expressing opinions

I believe that …
I disagree with the idea that …
I think that …
In my opinion, …
It is best not to …

The brain

concentrate
create an association
dementia
focus on a task
make a link
memory
mental illness
nerve connection/ending
neurobiologist
pain receptor
pick out information
relevant/irrelevant

Learning

bilingual
confused
creativity
distracted
inhibit learning
intellectual growth
monolingual
skills and knowledge
stress and anxiety

Types of intelligence

bodily/kinaesthetic intelligence
existential intelligence
interpersonal intelligence
intrapersonal intelligence
IQ
logical/mathematical intelligence
musical/rhythmic intelligence
naturalist intelligence
verbal/linguistic intelligence
visual/spatial intelligence

Understanding the world

act things out
analyse statistics
calculate
cause and effect
co-operate (with)
empathise (with)
features of the natural world
hands-on learning
in search of answers
keep a diary
keep time
learn song lyrics
melody and rhythm
memorise facts
pose and ponder questions
read a map/chart
recognise patterns
set a goal
show concern (for)
socialise
solve a problem
tell the difference between
(the) spatial world
underlying principles
think in visuals

School

academic
achievement
assembly
attendance
boarding school
cafeteria/tuckshop/refectory/
lunchroom
co-educational
corporal punishment
coursework
curricular activity
curriculum
day school
deadline
discipline
extracurricular activity
hand in work on time
head teacher
interactive
lecture
optional subject
private tutor
punish/punishment
qualification
rote learning
school leaving certificate
senior school
term/semester
timetable
uniform
vocational

Schooling in the past

ancestor
chant
hermitage
hieroglyphics
master
papyrus
scriptures

Describing things

inadequate
obsolete
old-fashioned
radical

Vocabulary: Chapter 5 – Competition

Competition
achievement
compete
drive someone to compete
enter a competition
judge (someone on something)
resounding success
victory

Reasons to compete
fulfilment
gain admiration/recognition
get knocked out
prize/reward
prove you are the best
push yourself to your limit
self-esteem
win a scholarship

Sport
audience
beat (someone on penalties)
break a world record
cross the finishing line
hold a tournament
host the World Cup
inter-regional championship
long-distance runner
lose in the first round
score a point
soccer
win a cup/gold medal

Nature
apex predator
compete for resources
conservation work
endangered
food chain
habitat
protected status
tag

Whales and sharks
attack
coastal waters
encircle
fatality
hunt
hunter
length
man-eater
migration pattern
pod
predator
predatory (fish)
prey
scientific survey
speed
weight

Talent shows
appear (on a show)
audition (for)
contest
encourage (someone to do something)
panel of judges
perform
performance
reduce someone to tears
solo

Buying a phone
antenna
app
(5-megapixel) camera
cloud storage backup
feature
handset
monthly subscription
predictive texting
(5-inch) screen
touchscreen
unlimited talk time/texts
vibrate function

Business
grow like wildfire
market leader
on the market
work overtime

Qualities
awesome
be hooked (on)
be obsessed with fame
harsh
have a reputation for (something)
have charisma
intent on success
powerful
pushy
responsive
ruthless
self-important
superior
temperate
waste of time

Making predictions
forecast
get something wrong
lay the foundation (for)
media coverage
outdoor pursuit

Work

earn/make money
get a (better) job
go straight to work
industry
work indoors/outdoors
work in a group/on
your own
work locally

Attributes, qualities and skills

be keen to learn
come up with something
confident
creative
embarrassed
get on with someone
have good people skills
independent
make a decision
managerial
take risks
talented
technical
turn ideas into reality
work on/with machinery

Talking about work and jobs

be in charge of a team
be rushed off your feet
drawbacks of a job

I haven't looked back!
interview
make a difference
rewards of a job
stressful
work regular hours

Jobs

architect
flexible/voluntary work
investor
journalist
Managing Director
part-time/full-time work
run your own business
(sales) assistant
self-employed
set up a business
software developer
start-up
supervisor
web designer
work experience
work for yourself
work placement

Preparing for work

design and technology
further education
specialise (in)
succeed in exams
train for a specific job
train on the job
training and qualifications

Applying for a job

achieve a goal
applicant
be available to start immediately
be suitable for the job
bring relevant knowledge to a job
candidate
competition for jobs
position/role
relevant experience/degree
vacancy

Working for start-ups

cockroach
digital hub
digital era
entrepreneur
funding
make a (steady) profit
unicorn

The Earth

fragile
harbour life
MEDC (more economically developed country)
outer space
worldwide

Environmental problems

air/sea/water/land pollution
carbon footprint
deforestation
disastrous effect (on)
environmental/global issue
freshwater (source)
habitat (destruction)
long-term consequences
plight
pollutant
pollute
pose a danger
tackle an issue
wellbeing

Humans and their activities

burn fossil fuels
car manufacture
economy
factory smoke
human being
(international) aviation
(international) shipping
leave a legacy
mankind
poacher
private/public transport
recreation and leisure
shrug your shoulders
sign of fertility
transportation

The greenhouse effect

absorb energy
atmosphere
carbon dioxide (emissions)
combustion
cool down
global warming
greenhouse gas (GHG)
heat up
infrared radiation
natural gas/methane
nitrous oxide
petroleum
sulphur dioxide
trap heat

The water crisis

acid rain
be parched
consumption
contamination
desalination plant
dump
fresh water supply
groundwater
human/industrial/agricultural waste
rainwater
sanitation
sewage
water table

Helping the environment

activist
assess
conservation
conservationist
conserve (water)
recycling (bin)
Red List
World Wildlife Fund

Air pollution

asthma
automobile exhaust
carbon monoxide (CO)
fatal
forest fire
heart disease
industrialised world
(lung) cancer
odourless (gas)
respiratory illness
smog

Wildlife

carnivore
cattle
decline/drop (in numbers)
densely populated
encroachment
(endangered) species
extinction
freshwater/marine creature
lay eggs
migrate
predator
trample (down) crops

Graphs and pie charts

bar graph
pie chart
statistic
x-axis
y-axis

Culture

artistic expression
belief
celebrate, celebration
community
cultural object
ethnic group
religion
street culture
the arts
traditional way of life

Art forms

African dance
ballet
calligraphy
carpet weaving
Fine Arts
hip hop
pottery
street dance
tap

Dance

agility
beauty
classical dance
coordination
grace
higher dance form
learn the basics
superhuman strength/ability
underground street culture

Mastery of an art

achieve mastery
evolve
get away with (less practice)
learn by heart
require practice
technique

Festivals

ceremonial ritual
display
festivities
fireworks
float
pageant
parade
procession
(rich) heritage
spectacular
take pride in
vibrant

The online world

addicted to (gaming)
addictive
gaming
headset
release a video
virtual reality
webcam

Opinions about art

admire
aggressive
dismiss (an idea)
form of aggression
inspirational
old-school
prize (something above something else)
reduce (dance to a mere show)
reject
revered (as an art)
status
valid

Travel

breathtaking (landscape)
countryside
historic
renowned
scenic
soak up the atmosphere
striking
take a dip/tour
temple
wander

Disappearing culture

abandon (a way of life)
death of a language
die out
mainstream society
minority language
nomadic/travelling community
overcrowding
preserve a culture
rural
urban
village lifestyle

Different ways to travel

air travel
airport
by car/bus/bike
canoe
cycle
go on a journey
in a short space of time
infrastructure
mass transport
method/mode of transport
motorway
on foot
overseas
pedestrian
set off on a journey
train/bus service
transport system
travel at speed
travel for leisure/pleasure

Trains

intercity railway
let off steam
(public) railway
railway mania
run on coal
steam locomotive
Trans-Siberian Railway
(the) underground

Inventions

create an opportunity
development
earlier models
influence our lives
shape (modern Britain)

Green travel

alternative transport
bamboo
carbon-fibre
green form of transport
heat-resistant
Hyperloop
made artificially
Passing Cloud
power of the wind
recycled material
sustainable
synthetic
Volocopter
waterproof
zero emissions

Space travel

carry passengers
communication satellite
gravity
launch pad
propel
rocket
shuttle programme
space exploration
space flight/station/tourism
spacecraft
telecommunications

Describing travelling

be unheard of
breathtaking
comfy seats
exceed my expectations
go on holiday
legendary

overlook the sea
palm tree
scenic
sightseeing
uncomfortable
unimpressive
vast

Travel on water

catch a ferry
(ferry) port
water taxi
waterway

Problems with transport

congestion
cost
damage the environment
dig up the countryside
environmentally friendly
expensive
not enough open spaces
petrol
pollution
progress
release dangerous gases
take for granted

Clothing and accessories

bandana
bell-bottom trousers
beret
cowboy boots
crinoline skirt
cut-off/ripped jeans
denim jacket
drainpipe/hipster trousers
flats
graduation cap/gown
item/piece of clothing
jewellery
jodhpurs
kilt
kimono
leotard
salwar kameez
sandals
sari
sarong
shoulder pads
sunglasses
wedding dress

Headwear

bonnet
crown
feathered/bowler/peaked hat
fur-lined hood
headdress
headscarf
helmet
tiara
turban
veil

Describing styles

appropriate
baggy
casual
classic
distinctive
extreme
fitted
flared

flowy skirt
fluro (fluorescent)
full-skirted
gathered/loose trousers
high-waisted
innovative
loose-/tight-fitting
low-slung
match (with)
must-have (outfit)
narrow trouser leg
pop/splash of colour
practical
sporty
structured
tapered
timeless
versatile
vibrant colour

Fashion

campaign
couture
flexible dress code
follow a trend
hairstyle
street style
style of dress

Silk

bale of silk
chrysalis
fabric
filament
larvae
loom
luxurious
rear silkworms
silk moth
Silk Road
silkworm
spin a cocoon
thread
trade route
trading link
weave silk

Materials

fur
ivory
lace
leather
nylon
precious stone
sandalwood

Giving fashion advice

… to die for!
accessorise an outfit
Check out …!
Get the new look!
Get yourself some … asap!

Sports fashion

black/brown belt
loose robe
martial arts
track pants

The fashion industry

cult of skinniness
craftsman
embroiderer
exploit animals
sweatshop
tailor
unfair wages

Fur

disrupt the food chain
fox
fur farm/ranch
fur trade
keep/upset the environmental balance
otter
pelt
raccoon dog

Entertainment

amuse yourself
favourite pastime

Music

choir
classical composer/music
jazz
music industry
orchestra
piece of music
relevant
track

Buying music

at the click of a mouse button
be covered by law
(be in favour of) file sharing
build up a fan base
consumer
contentious issue
copyright law
criminal act
download music/a song
illegal
(independent) band
songwriter

Making music

band practice
cello
computer program
guitar
karaoke
on stage
perform
produce music
professional-sounding
reinvent (classical ideas)
take part (in an orchestra/ a choir)
venue
violin
wow an audience

Books

can't put (a book) down
drama
fiction
graphic novel
historical fiction
horror
non-fiction
poetry
reading habits
romance
science fiction
short story
textbook
thriller

TV

award-winning
breaking/in-depth news
catch up on the news
charts programme
chat show
correspondent
current affairs
documentary
educational
entertainment programme
football highlights
host
investigative news programme
keep someone informed
(monthly) subscription
natural history programme
popularise
redundant
repeat
satellite TV
soap opera
the news
TV listing
TV-watching habits
worthless entertainment

Making films

budget
director
edit
film critic
film industry
film-making
on location
(romance) scene
shoot/record/make a film
studio

Talking about films

action-packed
all-singing, all-dancing
all-time best/great movie
biggest grossing film
deadly dull
fight scene
jaw-dropping
laugh-out-loud
must-see
nerve-wracking
slow-moving
star rating
star-studded

Age and stages of life

adulthood
adolescence
at any age
become an adult
be employed
be in my (nineties)
be new to something
be treated like an adult
childhood (experiences)
citizen
coming-of-age ceremony
expectation
freedom
get/grow older
great-grandmother
infancy
initiation (into adulthood)
leave home
live to be (100)
marriage
mature
move out
over the age of (65)
ritual
save up money
shape your own future
stage of life
start a family
youth

Politics

access to (education)
account for
be at stake
be involved/play a part in
decisions
decision-making (ability)
engage with (a topic)
government
hold power
job creation
lower the voting age (to 16)
make an informed decision
minimum voting age
socially/economically/politically active
(the) political process
threat
viewpoint
vote
voting rights/system
worldview

Society

fast-growing/working-age population
gender
isolation
level of education
pay taxes
(respectable) member of society
rights and responsibilities
(younger/older) generation

Feelings and characteristics

affection
conscientious
courteous
inadequacy
regret

Learning and achievement

fulfil an ambition
(gradual) process
learning tool
record-breaking
talent (for)
teach an old dog new tricks

Numbers and statistics

below the average
between the ages of (15) and (24)
decrease (steeply)
improve (significantly)
percentage
proportion
under the age of (15)

Technology

blogger
cyber superstar
messaging
web-illiterate
wireless connection

Answers

Revision checks

Chapter	Reading	Writing	Speaking	Listening
1 Technology	2 web browser, application, equipment, machine	2 text message, email, video, calendar, reminder	1 storage, backup, file transfer, sync files, access data	2 upload, absorb, emit, demonstrate, crash
2 Exploration	1 Nouns: discovery, explorer, journey, territory Adjectives: hazardous, remote, mesmerising, accessible	1 on, to, –, –, for, on, of (–, no preposition needed) 2 gaze at the stars, face danger, generate electricity, declare something a success, crease the paper	–	1 Nouns: landscape, region, mineral deposits, deforestation Adjectives: unexplored, ambitious, illegal, arctic
3 Health	–	–	2 proteins, carbohydrates, oils and fats, vitamins, minerals	2 brown, simmer, season, serve, flavour
4 Education	2 timetable, attendance, coursework, discipline, qualification, curriculum 3 association – link; distracted – preoccupied; concentrate – focus; irrelevant – not connected; pain receptor – nerve ending	–	–	2 socialise, analyse, calculate, memorise, recognise, punish
5 Competition	–	2 audience, achievement, victory, media coverage, fulfilment, scholarship	–	1 touchscreen, antenna, feature, handset, subscription, predictive texting
6 Work	2 managing director, web designer, supervisor, self-employed, flexible work	–	–	1 up, with, take, up, run, off 2 investor, entrepreneur, industry, funding, profit

7 Environment and wildlife	1 carbon footprint, recycling bin, global warming, emissions, greenhouse gas, deforestation, methane	2 freshwater source, contamination, industrial waste, plight, desalination plant	–	2 conservationist, activist, carnivore, predator, poacher
8 Culture and society	–	2 festivities, procession, parade, fireworks, pageant, float	2 calligraphy, ballet, carpet weaving, Fine Arts	1 evolve, admire, dismiss, reject, revered
9 Transport	2 air travel, bus service, transport system, inner-city railway, steam locomotive, communications satellite	1 gravity: it is a noun 2 sightseeing, ferry port, palm tree, water taxi, waterway	2 congestion, spacecraft, infrastructure, pedestrian, launch pad, petrol	–
10 Fashion	1 bale of silk, fabric, loom, silkworm, spin a cocoon, thread, trade route, weave silk	1 On your feet: cowboy boots, flats, sandals; On your head: bandana, beret, graduation cap; On your body: bell-bottom trousers, denim jacket, ripped jeans	2 classic, distinctive, extreme, innovative, timeless, versatile	2 Jobs: tailor, craftsman, embroiderer; Materials: lace, leather, nylon; Animals: fox, otter, raccoon dog
11 Entertainment	–	1 graphic novel, romance, thriller, non-fiction, drama, science fiction, historical fiction, poetry, horror	1 dance programme, football highlights, charts programme, chat show, documentary, natural history programme, film, the news, soap opera	–
12 Young and old	2 infancy, adolescence, youth, adulthood, old age	1 do an informed decision is incorrect: the correct phrase is 'make an informed decision' 2 blogger, cyber superstar, messaging, web-illiterate, wireless connection	–	2 marriage, government, isolation, inadequacy, percentage

Chapter tests

1 Technology [Total: 36 marks]

1. **b)** Suggested answers:
   1. <u>What</u> is a <u>self-driving car</u>? [1]
   2. Find <u>three synonyms</u> for '<u>self-driving</u>' in the text. [1]
   3. <u>What</u> are the <u>advantages</u> and <u>disadvantages</u> of <u>self-driving cars</u>? [1]
   4. <u>Why</u> might we need <u>more time</u> to <u>prepare</u> <u>before</u> we use <u>self-driving cars on the roads</u>? [1]

   c) 1. a robotic car that does not need a driver [1]
   2. robotic, driverless, automatic [3]
   3. Advantages: they are cheaper to make and use than our current cars; they allow more people to 'drive', e.g. young people and disabled people; they could help to reduce accidents; they could help find parking solutions; they could give people more time to work or relax. Disadvantages: they would require changes in the law; many social changes would be needed; people would need to be prepared to lose the fun aspect of driving; people whose careers involve driving would lose their job; people would have to be sure they could trust a computer; criminals could use the technology for terrorism. [11]
   4. We are not ready because there are still so many disadvantages. [1]

2. **a)** You can expect to hear the names of people, of places in Africa, and of companies that have invested in Africa.

   1. names of places: Africa, Nairobi, Kenya
      names of people: President Kenyatta
      names of companies: IBM, Microsoft [6]
   2. words and phrases related to technology: technology-focused, mobile phones, internet, tech-companies, apps, access to technology, technological solutions [7]

   b) Suggested summary:
   Large tech companies have invested in Africa because of economic growth and better access to technology. This is something that President Kenyatta has welcomed. Both IBM and Microsoft have departments in Kenya. The African people benefit from the research that is done to find technological solutions to African problems and enjoy economic development. The companies themselves benefit as more people are able to buy their products. [3]

2 Exploration [Total: 44 marks]

1. Possible answers:
   a) astronaut, Mars, space agency, space capsule, space programme, stars, unmanned mission [5]
   b) armada, crew, cabin, deap sea exploration, underwater exploration, fleet, ice cutter, junk, patrol boat, pirate, port, sailor, scuba diving, shipwreck, voyage, warship [6]

2. The following should be ticked:
   - She greets the audience.
   - She says what she is going to talk about.
   - She uses a rhetorical question.
   - She uses the pronoun 'we'.
   - She uses facts. [5]

3. Underline and highlight as follows: [8]

	Underline …	Highlight …
a)	Successful oil companies make money	that does not mean that we need to worry about their activities
b)	Craters on the Moon and on Mars have been named after Magellan	which proves he is the most important explorer in history
c)	he was killed with a spear before his ship returned to Spain	I think we can say that Magellan was the first to go around the world
d)	• Sometimes people say that Magellan was Spanish • in fact, he was born in Portugal	–

4.

Oil exploration	The sea	Precious goods
drill	armada	ivory
flare	cabin	laquerware
leak	crew	pearls
well	pirate	porcelain

[12]

5. a) short
   b) sentences
   c) personal
   d) listening
   e) fact
   f) before
   g) gaps
   h) grammatically [8]

3 Health [Total: 53 marks]

1. Suggested answers:
   a) (any four:) to add, to boil, to bring to the boil, to brown, to chop, to cook, to crush, to flavour, to fry, to lower/reduce the heat, to mix, to season, to serve, to simmer, to stir [4]
   b) (any four:) tbsp/tablespoon, tsp/teaspoon, g/gram, kg/kilogram, ml/millilitre [4]
   c) (any four:) Who?: a person or the name of a person; What?: an object, event, idea or fact; When?: a time or date; Where?: a place or the name of a place: Why? a reason [4]

2.

Food	Health problems
dairy	diabetes
fortified cereal	fatigue
junk food	obesity
nuts	vaccine
poultry	weakness

[10]

3. a) do
   b) do
   c) do
   d) play
   e) play
   f) go
   g) do
   h) go
   i) go [9]

a) but
b) or
c) so
d) and [4]

a) Suggested answer (no marks awarded for this): The numbers are likely to be statistics about world poverty, e.g. how many people in the world are poor, or how the situation is changing.
two point two billion / 2.2 billion / 2 200 000 000 [2]
three dollars and ten cents / $3.10 / 3.10 USD [2]
eighty per cent / 80 per cent / 80% [2]
three hundred and eighty nine million / 389 million / 389 000 000 [2]

b) 1. **Simple sentences (any one)** [3]
- *The most important global issue is poverty.*
- *Have a look at the slides.*
- *Nearly 80 per cent of the extremely poor live in South Asia and Sub-Saharan Africa.*
- *That's 389 million people.*
- *This is a sad and worrying situation with severe consequences for the world as a whole.*
Compound sentence: *There are many issues facing the world today, but I can confidently say that there is one that is particularly relevant.*
Complex sentence: *The situation is worrying because 2.2 billion people live on less than the equivalent of $3.10 a day.*

2. **Simple sentences:** short, clear and informative, and therefore powerful
Compound sentences: The second part of the sentence (after 'but') is as important as the first part, and it gives further, different information from what was said before.
Complex sentences: give more detail; they provide evidence for the argument. [3]

3. The use of all three types of sentence structure makes the text more fluent, varied and interesting. [1]

c) 1. Longest noun phrase: *This is a sad and worrying situation with severe consequences for the world as a whole.* Noun phrases add variety and detail to a text. The detail can make a statement more persuasive. [2]
2. Abstract nouns (any one): issues, poverty, situation, equivalent, day, consequences [1]

4 Education [Total: 31 marks]
1. a) educated
b) career
c) learn
d) writing
e) skills
f) master
g) punished [7]

2. Suggested answers: [8]
b) Schools should help people to get ready for their future jobs. Schools ought to help students get ready for the world of work.
c) Chemistry should not be compulsory in school. Chemistry should be an optional subject.
d) Education has changed dramatically since ancient times. Education is very different from what it used to be in the olden days.
e) There is more to school than simply learning. Schools have many functions; they are not only about learning.

3. Suggested answers: [5]
b) She should have asked the teacher to help her.
c) I am sorry I can't say yes to that at the moment.
d) The show will start soon.
e) We had to turn down the idea for many reasons.
f) Say sorry to your grandma at once.

4. a) Suggested answers: [4]
1. noun: a word that refers to a person, thing or idea
2. verb: a word that expresses an action or a state
3. adjective: word that describes a noun
4. adverb: word that adds information about an action

b) Possible answers:
1. nouns: (any four) brain, water, pounds, pain receptors, nerve endings, pain, memory, associations, idea, apple, life, word, letter, picture, language, children, characters, symbols, links, age, structure [2]
2. verbs: (any four) did (you) know, is made up, weighs, means, (may) think, are experiencing, (can) feel, is formed, promote, studying, create, linking, learn, can be done, will make, have [2]
3. adjectives: similar, different [1]
4. adverbs: (any four) strangely, absolutely, early, probably, remarkably [2]

5 Competition [Total: 22 marks]
1. a) Suggested answers: [5]
Exams are seriously stressful!
They're an important part of your education and help determine the direction your life will take.
One of our greatest fears is failure.
Four whole years of training go into an Olympic performance. (includes a number)
… you can change the way you think. World class athletes know this.
These athletes are nervous … but confident
Elite performers expect to succeed …
They go out there ready to show the world what they can do.
Sport psychology is used to help athletes cope …
A large proportion of an athlete's training is mental.
I'm going to discuss two things: … (includes a number)

b) Suggested answer: [1]
… you can learn how to respond successfully to the stress of taking exams.

c) and, but, or, so [4]

2. a) Suggested answer: [4]
Exams are seriously stressful! … This can shake your confidence pretty badly, make you feel nervous and make taking an exam a bit more difficult. // The great news is that you can change the way you think. World class athletes know this. … Elite performers expect to succeed; they don't try not to fail! They go out there ready to show the world what they can do. // Sport psychology is used to help athletes cope with these enormous pressures, putting all their energy into a winning performance. A large proportion of an athlete's training is mental. Just like those world class athletes, you can learn how to respond successfully to the stress of taking exams. // So, to successfully control exam nerves, I'm going to discuss two things: firstly how and why we get nervous, and secondly, coping strategies to reduce anxiety levels and build your confidence. //

b) People are naturally scared of failure, and exams are stressful because they influence our lives. We can learn from athletes how to be less nervous: they know how to cope with stress and they use sports psychology to be more confident about winning. [4]

3. a) Options 2) and 3) are good answers because they develop the response. Option 1) is too short; option 4) is not a relevant answer to the question.
    b) Options 1) and 4) are good answers because they develop the response. Option 2) is too short; option 3) is not a relevant answer to the question (listening to music is different from playing it). [4]

6 Work [Total: 7 marks]

1. a) Possible headings: Attitude 1; Attitude 2; Creating success

    [no marks]

    d) Possible answers: [no marks]

    Definition mindset: attitude to life

    Attitude 1: fixed mindset; What? fear failure, scared to work hard; Why? parents/teachers have praised too much; Consequences: avoid challenges, give up

    Attitude 2: growth mindset; What? look positively on challenges, see failure as opportunity; Consequences: satisfaction from success, happy to learn from failure, happier

    Creating success: work at a growth mindset

    e) 1. It is your attitude to life (e.g. study, work). [1]

    2. People with a fixed mindset fear failure; people with a growth mindset learn from failure. [2]

    3. They were praised too much when they were little. [1]

    4. You should adopt a growth mindset because you get satisfaction from success, and failure is not a problem. A growth mindset also makes you happier. [2]

    5. It would probably be difficult to make changes, but it is worth it. [1]

7 Environment and wildlife [Total: 40 marks]

1. Suggested answers:
    1. conservationist, activist [2]
    2. (any four) acid rain, air/water/land pollution, deforestation, endangered species, extinction of species, forest fires, global warming, habitat destruction, human/industrial/agricultural waste, poisoned water, sewage, water contamination [4]

2. a) recycle
    b) collect
    c) treat
    d) works
    e) do you do
    f) get
    g) has
    h) collect
    i) bring
    j) is not
    k) am doing
    l) am sorting
    m) am putting
    n) do [14]

3. a) (any ten) extraordinary, fascinated, astonishing, terrified, shocked, enormous, drenched, thrilled, incredible, nervous, energising, peaceful, emotional [10]

    b) I first saw a real one; the most astonishing thing I'd ever seen; I felt terrified and shocked; I'd not expected to see it practically face to face; I could taste the salty water; I started feeling numb with cold; I did feel nervous; I couldn't see anything; I could feel my heart beating; I've never felt more emotional [10]

8 Culture and society [Total: 47 marks]

1. a) calligraphy
    b) pottery
    c) ballet
    d) hip hop
    e) culture [5]

2. a) Text 1 [24]

> Hip hop and street dance might be popular at the local club but they shouldn't be welcomed as an art dance form at a national dance competition. There's far too much of it in competitions nowadays. Forms of dance such as ballet and tap have a long and creditable history and require hours and hours of practice to achieve high levels of technique and mastery. Hip hop does not require this level of practice and cannot be compared to these other higher dance forms. Hip hop's obsession with tricks like balancing on your head reduces dance to mere show and not art. Dance should be about grace, beauty and culture.
> There has been too much encouragement of hip hop and, dance schools and competitions like this one should be encouraging young people to learn the basics of dance through concentrating on classical dance.

Text 2

> You obviously don't know what you're talking about! Street dance is just as valid as classical dance and they deserved to win. Two years ago I met a lot of hip hop dancers who all belonged to an underground street culture – all with superhuman strength and abilities. They could fly in the air. They could bend their elbows all the way back. They could spin on their heads 80 times in a row.
> Our new dancers come from hip hop and street culture. Dance is changing and evolving and people need to realise that. Online videos and social networking between dancers have created a global laboratory online for dance. I've seen kids in Japan take moves from a YouTube video created in Detroit, copy it, change it within days, and release a new video. And this is happening every day. And from bedrooms and living rooms and garages, with cheap webcams, will come the world's great dancers of tomorrow. And because these dancers can now talk across different continents, hip hop will transform dance and change the world.

    b) 1. Text 1: *Hip hop and street dance might be popular at the local club* is a positive statement about hip hop. The writer uses 'might' to acknowledge a different point of view, before saying that hip hop is not art. [2]
    2. Text 2: The speaker says that *hip hop will transform dance and change the world.* The reason is *because these dancers can now talk across different continents.* [2]

    c) Text 1: 1 require 2 achieve 3 mere
       Text 2: 4 superhuman 5 spin 6 realise 7 created 8 transform [8]

3. Suggested answers:
    a) What are the reasons for this?
    b) Why is dance a really important art form?
    c) How can this problem be solved?
    d) How often does this happen?
    e) Is this a good enough reason?
    f) What should dance schools do instead? [6]

Transport [Total: 44 marks]

1.
   1. c
   2. f
   3. g
   4. e
   5. a
   6. d
   7. b   [7]

2.
   1. c: The other statements say nothing about exercise, but about being in or out of a house.
   2. a: The other sentences refer to the minimum amount of exercise; this one is about the maximum.
   3. c: The other sentences refer to the use of public transport in urban locations.   [6]

3.
   a) are
   b) drive
   c) have
   d) goes
   e) were/used to be
   f) costs
   g) will get
   h) don't cause   [8]

4.
   a) where
   b) even though
   c) should
   d) that
   e) can
   f) who
   g) because
   h) when   [8]

5. Possible answers:
   a) space exploration, space flight, space station, space tourism   [4]
   b) (any three) who, which that, where, when, whose   [3]
   c) (any two) go on a journey, take a trip, set off on a journey   [2]
   d) breathtaking, scenic, unimpressive   [3]
   e) (any three) and, but, or, so, because, as, since, although, even though [3]

10 Fashion [Total: 23 marks]

1. Different information is underlined; text not in the flow chart is highlighted.   [7]

> If you would like to apply online for our 'Fashion for beginners' course, you will need to follow a six-step process. First of all, you will need to gather all your documents. Please refer to the checklist on the next page to make sure you have them all. You will need to scan these. Then go to the application web page, click here, to fill in a short form and submit your scanned documents. All applicants will be granted an interview, face to face or by Skype or phone. There are three possible outcomes: successful, unsuccessful, or you will be placed on a waiting list. If you are offered a place, you will need to let us know in writing, within two weeks, whether you accept the offer or not.

2.
   1. d
   2. e
   3. b
   4. a
   5. g
   6. c
   7. f   [7]

3.
   a) the best
   b) the hardest (and) most talented
   c) larger
   d) the greatest
   e) the oldest
   f) more supportive (or) kinder
   g) better   [9]

11 Entertainment [Total: 34 marks]

1. Possible answers:
   a) (any five) action-packed, all-singing, all-dancing, astonishing, awesome, deadly dull, gripping, jaw-dropping, laugh-out-loud, nerve-wracking, slow-moving, thrilling   [5]
   b) (any four) graphic fiction, historical fiction, horror, romance, science fiction, thriller   [4]
   c) (any six) charts programme, chat show, current affairs programme, dance programme, documentary, educational programme, entertainment programme, football highlights programme, investigative news programme, natural history programme, news programme, soap opera, the news   [6]

2.
   a) 1. Sorry, Kate, but I was wondering if you know what the numbers are – how many people are using them?
      2. Yes, of course, we can talk about those, and we can compare the benefits of both.
      3. Yes, when you're travelling, it's better to take something light. I have to say that that's the only advantage for me, though. I still prefer books all other times.
      4. Yes, they're great for disabled people and they have more functions, but for me a printed book is more than enough to keep me happy.
      5. Yes, they're something you can hold, …   [5]

   b) 1. That's a good idea, but I think …
      2. I see what you're saying but …
      3. I take your point, Hannah, but …
      4. I'm not sure that's the only advantage.
      5. Perhaps, but …   [5]

3. On Friday 12 October, we held several class discussions about a variety of topics. As I am really interested in literature, I have chosen to write about the group that discussed the topic of e-readers. There were three participants in this group: [1] Kate, Josh and Hannah. Kate, [1] who had been chosen to lead the debate, [1] started by thanking the audience and by defining e-readers. In the discussion, Kate seemed to prefer e-readers, but Josh said, 'I still prefer books,' [2] even though he agreed they were useful when travelling. Hannah, [1] the third group member, [1] admitted that e-readers were functional and useful but personally, she preferred books as they were physical. I can't [1] tell you who won the argument on the day, but I can say that it was very interesting for everyone concerned and that the participants' [1] contributions were highly valued by the audience.   [9]

12 Young and old [Total: 14 marks]

1. a) become
    b) live
    c) get
    d) shape
    e) leave
    f) treat
    g) save up
    h) start   [8]

2. Suggested answers:
    a) He works as an architect in a large company.
    b) My guess is that great-grandma is ninety-one or ninety-two.
    c) Joe had asthma when he was a baby.
    d) Scientists don't often work alone; they usually work with other scientists.
    e) The cost of TVs has gone down a lot.
    f) Mr Barrett can't use a computer.   [6]

3. b)

Transcript: Extract from an interview

Interviewer: Could you tell me a bit more about the 'Being-a-Friend' organisation?

Rita: Well, Being-a-Friend brings people from all ages and walks of life together. People contact the organisation if they feel they'd like to have more people in their lives, and volunteers go [emphasis] and befriend [emphasis] them. We mainly work in cities, but people from all [emphasis] over the country can access the service.

Interviewer: And what's your role?

Rita: I'm one of the volunteers working with the elderly in Manchester. At the moment, I regularly visit three people, all over the age of 70, in their homes.

Interviewer: And what do you do for these people?

Rita: I don't do [emphasis] much, really. Sometimes something practical needs to be done, and I might do some shopping for them, [pause] but my main [emphasis] role is to spend time [emphasis] with them, [pause] listen [emphasis] to them, [pause] just be a good friend.

Interviewer: What do you think about the work that 'Being-a-Friend' does?

Rita: I think it's very [emphasis] important. I've only been with the organisation for two years, but in that time I've realised that many of the people I've visited don't see anybody else all week – just me [emphasis]. If the organisation wasn't there for them, they'd be very [emphasis] lonely. It's easy to get isolated. Very often, relatives move out or away, and people are left on their own. They don't like to cook just for themselves and they might not have friends who live nearby. It's what happens in cities. And then soon, [pause] they stop taking proper care of themselves. They stop being active altogether. That can have a negative [emphasis] impact on their health and how they feel [emphasis] about life. So having a friend from the organisation visit them can make a big [emphasis] difference to what they get out of life.

Interviewer: And that's why you volunteer? To make people's lives better?

Rita: Yes and no. Of course, [increase in volume] it's lovely if people tell you they've had a great day or that they've really enjoyed an activity we did together. We often go to the shops, visit a garden centre, have a cup of tea … But that's not the only [emphasis] reason I do it. These people have had lives [emphasis], they've had jobs [emphasis], they've had families [emphasis]. There have been amazing [emphasis] changes over their lifetimes. They have lots [emphasis] of interesting stories to tell. I like listening to people telling me about how different their lives used to be, and I always ask them what their opinions are about the way we do things now. [pause] I learn [emphasis] so much from them.

Interviewer: Any final thoughts?

Rita: Erm, I'm not sure. [pause] Yes. [increase in volume] There is [emphasis] something. I just want to say that I want to be like that, you know? I'm nearly 18 now, but when I'm as old as these friends, I want to be just like them: [emphasis] full of interesting stories and happy to give advice to younger people.

Interviewer: Thank you for your time.

Rita: You're welcome!

Notes